THE *ASTONISHING LIVES* OF *OLDER WOMEN*

THE *ASTONISHING LIVES* OF *OLDER WOMEN*

HOW TO CREATE PLEASURE OVER PERIL IN PEAK LONGEVITY

MOIRA WELSH

ECW

Published by ECW Press
665 Gerrard Street East
Toronto, Ontario, Canada M4M 1Y2
416-694-3348 / info@ecwpress.com

Editor for the Press: Pia Singhal
Copy editor: Crissy Boylan
Cover design: Jess Albert

LIBRARY AND ARCHIVES CANADA CATALOGUING IN PUBLICATION

Title: The astonishing lives of older women : how to create pleasure over peril in peak longevity / Moira Welsh.

Names: Welsh, Moira, author.

Description: Includes bibliographical references.

Identifiers: Canadiana (print) 20250321238 | Canadiana (ebook) 20250321300

ISBN 978-1-77041-800-4 (softcover)
ISBN 978-1-77852-535-3 (ePub)
ISBN 978-1-77852-536-0 (PDF)

Subjects: LCSH: Older women—Economic conditions. | LCSH: Older women—Social conditions.

Classification: LCC HQ1063.7 .W45 2026 | DDC 305.26/2—dc23

This book is funded in part by the Government of Canada. *Ce livre est financé en partie par le gouvernement du Canada.* We acknowledge the support of the Canada Council for the Arts. *Nous remercions le Conseil des arts du Canada de son soutien.* We would like to acknowledge the funding support of the Ontario Arts Council (OAC) and the Government of Ontario for their support. We also acknowledge the support of the Government of Ontario through the Ontario Book Publishing Tax Credit, and through Ontario Creates.

PRINTED AND BOUND IN CANADA

PRINTING: MARQUIS 5 4 3 2 1

Contents

Introduction

Life comes at you fast.

As women, it propels us through careers, sleepless years of early motherhood, the insomnia of raising teenagers and after our children launch, a marriage dissolves or a job reaches its finale, we shoot out the other end, often unprepared for the decades ahead.

When you are in the thick of it, who has time to think about how you will live at 65? Or 80? Or, for that matter, 100? Centenarians are one of Canada's fastest-growing demographics. More women will reach that big birthday or come close — a new reality that can transform, in positive ways, our view of aging.

And yet the stories of women in this book are alarming. Infuriating. And depending on their personal finances, terrifying. They scare my 28-year-old son, who, as a business-school graduate working in a male-dominated industry, appears personally immune to such problems but to him their experience is distressing.

Older women fade into the shadows and not by choice. Society doesn't much know what to do with women in their

70s or 80s, long past the mothering years. Of course, there are fabulous exceptions, but many grow accustomed to the averted gaze, and older men do too.

It is worse for women without money. Some feel shame at this final stretch into impoverishment, even though at least part of it was predictable. Once you know why, it's hard to look away.

In the coming pages, I describe how life took unexpected turns for three women who entered adulthood in the 1960s with great optimism promised from an education, a husband, and, soon enough, children. Admittedly, one was a free spirit. The other two joined the robust middle class. A house with stained-glass windows. A yacht. Interesting but not lucrative jobs that began as children grew. Now close to 80 or beyond, the stories of Pat, Susan, and Elizabeth offer a brutally honest warning about money and old age, a harsh survival that none imagined all those years ago.

While this sounds bleak, there is also much hope. We are entering a period that could witness the rise of older women, including those with power who are already using their voices to talk about aging with fresh plans and panache. Women in their 80s, such as actor and activist Jane Fonda, are discussing the sustaining joys of female friendship, a wonderful gift. Ninety-four-year-old Inge Fowlie, a celebrity in her Toronto friend circle, is reclaiming the word *crone* as a symbol of female power and sensuality. A new collective focus on well-being means that middle age can stretch into our 60s and even 70s, at least for those who can afford it.

We are all aging, and that is okay. Apparently, there is much to anticipate. In this book, some share stories about fabulous octogenarian sex, a topic, I discovered, that older women greatly enjoy discussing. Love can surprise us later in life, as evidenced by the photos a friend showed me at a cocktail party, her mother wrapped in the arms of a handsome white-haired man she met online, a man she proclaimed was the love of her life. Sometimes we do get our big romance, even if it arrives in our 80s. In these pages, you will meet women who were happily married until a partner died and later chose a new person, living apart but enjoying the benefits. We will explore these courtships, a second or fourth chance at love that can last until the end of days. Statistically speaking, it is the men who depart first, on average at the age of 79.5, roughly four years younger than women.

In many ways, untimely male exodus aside, the world of aging is brimming with good news.

Let us consider longevity. For Canadians born in 1901, the average life expectancy was roughly 50; today, many will get an additional three or four decades, if not more. Americans will, too, though their average lifespan is slightly shorter. Those who outlive expectations will mostly be women. As society and as individuals, we are just starting to ponder the meaning of these extra decades, an opportunity to start afresh or, less happily, the grim thrash of survival.

The goal of this book is to help women chart a forward course by sharing both uplifting and cautionary tales, so that we can prepare for the potentially exciting time that lies ahead. I also provide financial fundamentals, which we often do not consider during the crush of careers and caring for busy kids or aging parents.

Mixed into tales of late-life romance and adventure is the reality check of hardship, created by the immutable gender pension gap, which is the difference in retirement income between women and men. Guess who comes out ahead.

We will hear wise words from professionals such as Leanne Kaufman, president and chief executive officer of RBC Royal

Trust, a powerful advocate whose partnerships include the Women's Age Lab, founded by groundbreaking geriatrician Dr. Paula Rochon, at Toronto's Women's College Hospital.

It is through Dr. Rochon's work that many women are now recognizing the inequities sharpened by a long life. While medical research is improving (at least in Canada), much of our knowledge is still based on studies of men, often younger men. As Dr. Rochon explains, women's bodies — and the bodies of older women in particular — are different.

Let's not lose sight of younger women who are immersed in the labour of life. Their perspective is told through the story of a 30-something writer for the famed Lainey Gossip website who gives her readers the hard facts on financial independence amid today's complicated relationships.

When I discuss this book with millennials, some seem surprised that in 2031, the eldest of their demographic will turn 50. For so long, we have equated millennials with eternal youth, but like all of us, they are on the inevitable march forward and can benefit from the learnings of those who came before them.

Mostly, this book is an homage to women in the late decades of life. We don't talk about them enough. There is a rich perspective in their knowledge, divined over time.

Many came of age just before or during the counterculture revolution of the 1960s, when the world tilted to meet the demands of youth. Due to their considerable numbers, that dominance continued as the postwar generation we now call boomers marched through life. Today, the sheer economic power of some 35 million women over the age of 65 in the United States and Canada offers us the potential to rebrand female longevity. This unprecedented period provides many new opportunities for exploration. The least examined is the lifelong desire for intimacy, the sexual freedom that can come with age.

It's hard to imagine what one day awaits. In the early years of motherhood, there are few opportunities to have a shower or an adult conversation without the well-timed interruptions of a toddler or teenager. Aloneness is a luxury. The freedom to read, hike, or dig peacefully in the garden is an imagined luxury. And yet, in a flash, that phase of life is over. Our children move out and sometimes spouses die or we decide we're better off without them. Suddenly, the pressures ease. (This may explain why longitudinal data says unmarried women with no children are the happiest and healthiest.)

There are many people whose marriages thrive through the years, a blessing, really, but for those whose relationships end, through death or disquiet, there can be wondrous value in feeling comfortable on your own. As they say on Instagram, "That shit is golden." But if solitude turns to isolation, it can lead to risks of the physical and cognitive kind. Dementia. Depression. Heart disease.

It is true that older women are at risk of loneliness, yearning for friends to sustain life or the sensual touch of another person that 94-year-old Inge says everyone craves until death. Her 91-year-old boyfriend died four years earlier, and sometimes, Inge says, when masturbating with the vibrator meant to replace a man, the absence of another human in her room is so stark that after climaxing, she cries.

To sharpen the pain of loneliness, many women live decades longer with significantly less money than our male cohorts, a prospect worsened by Canada's desperate lack of affordable housing. This confluence of events is the modern, gendered version of old-age impoverishment.

To be fair to Canadian policy-makers, the benefits of the Canada Pension Plan, Old Age Security, and the Guaranteed Income Security are praised internationally for success in lowering the official poverty rate among those aged 65 and older to between 5 and 6 percent, though that percentage more than doubles for those living alone.

While writing this book, I heard from learned people who cited these glowing statistics, inferring that I was wasting my time. I disagree. But trying to quantify just how many older women are living in financial stress can lead to a descent into a proverbial rabbit hole, in this case a numerically abstract abyss of official definitions that frankly don't reflect modern conditions.

As wealth and precarity grow ever apart, it is hard to precisely say how many women are falling behind or one day likely will. In many ways, their lives go unmeasured and unmanaged, invisible to policy-makers, although as Canadian poverty researcher Dr. Amanda Grenier says, "When does it become enough people for us to say it is a problem?"

Most of the women I interviewed for this book do not fit Canada's official poverty measurement, which, some academics allege, was chosen for its relatively rosy outcomes. While not officially destitute, many women are deeply stressed by life's unaffordability.

When I shared this observation with Alexi White, of the research-focused foundation Maytree, he had an immediate reaction: "Part of the problem with the way that we colloquially talk about the poverty line is that people think that it's some kind of measure of like, 'If you're below the poverty line, you have trouble surviving. If you're above the poverty line, you don't.' And that's complete garbage."

While there is great value in celebrating the remarkable gains of women in education and professions, it is also true that not all qualify for a high-salary career with a lifelong pension. Some won't attain the education needed to get public sector benefits as a teacher or nurse, let alone to become a computer science grad earning $300,000 a year working remotely for Google.

Unlike the pension gap, the gender pay gap is slowly closing. However, there is another truth that a report commissioned by the Pay Equity Office of Ontario (PEO) takes pains to share: Even if salary disparities ended tomorrow, the benefits would not mitigate the challenge of an employment and pension system designed to reflect the lives of men. The PEO report calls this "male-pattern employment."

We will go into sharp detail on these points, including the motherhood penalty, in Chapter Ten, which also offers a quick history of the mid-twentieth century's impact on women's retirement today and a feminist economist's advice on marriage.

Old age, writ large, is coming. In 2050, the number of Canadians past their 65th birthday is expected to hit 12 million, so after decades of declining workplace pensions and rising short-term gig jobs, Gen X and millennials may wish to take heed.

Young people who cannot afford the benefits of home ownership could end up working long past the traditional retirement age. It's hard to meet the standards of so-called retirement readiness when rent (or massive mortgages for the lucky ones) leave little money for savings. Inheritance might help, especially from the real estate value of parents' homes, except the flip side of longevity means many older Canadians will dip into that equity to pay for the cost of long lives. It is worth considering these points when making decisions on careers, employer generosity, or the spending patterns of a future partner.

As for the enormous baby boomer generation now reaching their 80s, there is great wealth among that demographic, but not everyone rode the wave. Some worked hard but did not make a lot of money. Many were renters. Not everyone married a spouse with a healthy pension, and not all survivors' benefits pay enough to make a difference on rent or property taxes.

Some women got divorced and, as single mothers, spent most of their money on their children. There is an inherent value to raising children who go on to thrive, but it comes with a financial cost. Add unaffordable housing to the mix, and it is women, in so many ways, whose older years turn to hell. It's easy to ignore, but their experience may one day be ours.

As a journalist who spent three years leading the *Toronto Star*'s Third Act project, focused on older adults, I published a story in early 2023 that examined the struggles of women, educated with meaningful careers, who found themselves shut out of affordable living options, not to mention *life*, in their 60s, 70s, and 80s. Many were widowed or divorced. Others never married, nor did they have children. Some had master's degrees. They had careers. What they didn't have was a job that provided wealth, a healthy workplace pension, or 40 years of paid employment over a certain salary threshold to qualify for the maximum Canada Pension Plan, even though CPP payments were never designed to be substantial.

In recent years, as housing costs reached levels that remain unaffordable, some older renters were hit with the dreaded word *renoviction*, the act of evicting a tenant to renovate that is often a sly way to increase rent. Many women are on this trajectory, even if they don't realize it. As I wrote in the *Star*, with each move, they disappear, lower and lower, into the basement.

Dr. Samir Sinha is a geriatrician who watches his patients, older women, move into these subterranean homes. He warns that as bodies grow frail, they'll be trapped by impassable stairs, the dark and depressing window light, the struggle of it all. They tell him this is their reality. There is nowhere else to go.

All of this speaks of a future that nobody wants, so we look away.

There is a painful truth in acknowledging that a great many women will spend their final decades in a version of deprivation that harms body and spirit. Surveys show that middle-aged Canadians fear financial survival in retirement; Gen Xers have started turning 60 and with millennials in hot pursuit, this trend won't end with the boomers.

By the early 2030s, nearly one in four Canadians will be old, at least by official standards. In two decades, we will enter our potentially frail years when roughly 2.5 million will be 85 or beyond, with twice as many women as men.

For the icing on the statistical cake, as many as 125,000 Canadians could become centenarians in 40 years, according to Statistics Canada's high growth scenario. In the United States, the number of centenarians is expected to surpass 400,000.

We are sitting on a demographic time bomb, and yet the struggles of older women, particularly those just above the official poverty line, are rarely discussed. These women are aging into a policy morass, growing increasingly vulnerable at an impossibly expensive time.

This version of aging-while-female is very real, while for others, particularly those blessed with financial stability, we are witnessing a shift toward empowerment.

Older celebrities are embracing their mature years, including high-profile names such as American actor Julia Louis-Dreyfus, whose wildly popular podcast, *Wiser Than Me*, examines aging, love, life, ambition, and female friendship with Sally Field, Gloria

Steinem, and Billie Jean King, all of whom have thoughts on the art of aging. These women are not financially struggling, not at all, but by speaking about women's bodies, aspirations, friendships, health, and, yes, sex lives, they have the potential to influence our later years.

If not consumed by financial survival, these extra decades can offer a renaissance of extraordinary expression. This can lead to fascinating conversations about new life purpose or fresh ideas about sexuality, perhaps a trend toward pragmatic polyamory as similarly aged men die and a new demographic of women take control, an idea that sparked many a lively conversation in my research.

Mostly, we are entering a period of great risk. As a country or continent, we are growing older by the millions. Women are living longer, with less. The curse of loneliness has attached itself to the gift of longevity, giving us more years to disappear into the basement.

GENDER GAP FACTS

The average gender pension gap among 34 countries is 26 percent, according to 2021 figures from the Organisation for Economic Co-operation and Development. Canada's gender pension gap was 22 percent. In the United States, it was nearly 34 percent.

Using a different measurement, the Pay Equity Office of Ontario (PEO) puts the pension gap at 17 percent, meaning that for every dollar a man earns in retirement, a woman gets 83 cents.

Canada's gender pay gap, the difference in annual income between men and women, is slowly closing, according to the PEO report. In 1997, it was 37 percent compared to 28 percent in 2021, an undeniable improvement but still far too wide.

CHAPTER ONE

Susan, Pat, and Elizabeth

Sometimes, living in a car is the only way a lady can survive.

At the age of 76, Susan Patricia Staples is a veteran of vehicle residency, as it is called, the act of sleeping in a car with no address except the next Walmart parking lot. She did it for nine impoverished months a few years ago, and if car life sounds like part of her past, it isn't. Sleeping in her vehicle is the only way she can afford to leave her tiny apartment and visit friends in faraway locales, staying connected to the world.

Car life, says Susan, is a pragmatic choice for women unable to afford housing in a time of impossible rental costs. While there is limited Canadian data, if any, on its prevalence, American researchers have given it much consideration because it is a way of life in the United States. Across North America, there are thriving online communities of women who have embraced this existence. They post photos of portable toilets and spacious sleeping hacks, such as tents that connect with the open door of their vehicle. On Facebook, women share their stories, which often involve a job loss or leaving a toxic partner, and receive dozens of supportive messages.

Sleeping in a vehicle is either a necessity or a subversive act of freedom, Susan says. "There are two reasons why we older women end up in cars. One is because we can't afford housing. The other is because we can't afford life."

Susan has the steady gaze of a woman who can hold her place in the world. Her hair is long and wavy, an elegant shade of grey that looks as if a stylist selected it, though Susan does not have the money, nor the inclination, for such proclivities.

Still, she does not look like someone who, in 2018, approaching the age of 70, lived in a Ford Focus with the rear seats removed. It had a makeshift bed on one side and on the other, boxes with shampoo, soap, toilet paper, clothes, and big plastic water bottles, as she explains, to wash private bits under billowing dresses while hidden behind trees in a park. As she tells other women, if you keep yourself presentable, no one will know.

Look around, look closely. You may see signs of this poverty, although women are discreet. Some still have the veneer of a middle-class life. This existence is not what these women imagined decades earlier when their children were young or the job opportunities seemed exciting, even if they did not pay well. The money will come later, they told themselves — except sometimes it doesn't. Sometimes those jobs are creatively satisfying or flexible enough to help accommodate parenting, but that work does not always lead to flush retirement savings or a livable pension.

Susan has a degree in social work from Carleton University in Ottawa. She raised a son, now in his late 30s, and for a time ran an after-school education program in a local church as a small-scale entrepreneur. She is admittedly a hippie at heart, or at least she was in her youth, but never imagined that during those nine months of hard-core car life, she would feel a glow of pride knowing that none of the parents knew the tutor slept in a parking lot.

These days, she has an old van. Susan doesn't have the money to buy airplane tickets, but she loves to be out in the world, to visit friends and go deep into discussions on politics, global affairs, or the value of existence with a body in decline. When she goes too long without these visits, Susan feels trapped. She's left with elevator small talk. Car life offers her an escape from her tiny, subsidized Ottawa apartment; it's the only way she can reach the source of her emotional sustenance. And that worries her the most. Susan expects to be among the growing cohort of women who live for a very long time. What if her apartment complex is sold to private developers? What if her body doesn't keep up with her mind? Once physical decline begins, can she live in her van or make those 20-hour trips? In quiet moments, she wonders if longevity is a blessing after all.

For now, she tries to avoid those thoughts and stays busy, sharing tips on the nuances of vehicle domesticity with women online.

On hot summer nights, she says, use netting attached to Velcro around the windows, allowing a breeze to float inside without bugs. A McDonald's restroom offers a quick early morning wash; just leave it clean. Sleep on a mattress of upholstery foam, instead of the memory kind, which is temperature sensitive and feels like a block of ice in the winter.

When Susan first started living in her car, few were publicly speaking about this peripatetic life, at least in Canada. It is better known in America, where the 2017 book *Nomadland* examined the lives of men and women who lost jobs in the 2008 depression and drove across the country, chasing work. It is, of course, anecdotal, but in the past few years, on private Facebook sites in Canada and the United States, Susan has noticed more women, especially older women, asking detailed questions about survival.

A women-only Facebook site devoted to car life and camping in North America has 122,000 members, though not everyone in the group relies on vehicles for housing. Many are curious. Others are considering the option as their savings run out. Some sleep in their cars to save money on travel, like Susan. Others say they have crossed over, like a 74-year-old woman with mobility issues who asked for advice on a portable stool for the back of her truck. In another post, one woman wrote, "When I turned 68, never in a million years did I think I would end up living in my van."

Sometimes talk turns to the judgment of others, the fear of exposure to problematic people or, equally dangerous, the cold. Some post heartfelt responses, often with advice on survival or warnings about certain states that have made it illegal to park overnight anywhere other than an official campsite. Others recommend the safety of Quartzsite, Arizona, a destination with long-established vehicle communities. Many are Americans, but on a Canadian Facebook chat group, women send each other messages mostly about safe parking lots or surviving subzero temperatures. Everyone has a solution for the cold. Susan zips together two extreme weather sleeping bags, slides inside and wraps a fleece Polar Plus blanket around her head before stuffing the rest of it around her shoulders and deep inside to fill the pockets of cold air.

However anecdotal, and it is, Susan sees a rise in the number of Canadian women posting pictures of solo life on the road or asking how to do it for financial survival. The struggle to afford housing and food is somewhat more quantifiable, with 80,000 Ontarians known to be homeless, at least for a time, in 2024, a number that could double by 2035. That does not include the hidden homeless, those who sleep on friends' couches or in cars.

While many older men are also living on a low income in a time of rising housing and food costs, it is women who are most at risk. In Canada, the gender pension gap, the difference in retirement savings and pensions meant to carry you through your final decades, ranges from 17 to 26 percent, depending on how it is measured. It's often higher for racialized women or those who immigrated to Canada as adults. The pension gap especially impacts women who worked part-time or had a low salary. The less you contribute to a pension, whether a workplace's or CPP, the lower the earnings in retirement.

Canada's gender pension gap has not narrowed in the 45 years between 1976 and 2021, and while younger women are increasingly educated and employed in jobs with workplace pensions, a great many are not, which places them on the direct path to precarity.

"It's a huge social problem," Susan says. "I have a lot of friends who are semi-professional, and there's not a lot of padding between them and poverty. I was a single mom. I spent all my money on my son, and we had a fantastic life. But I have no savings."

It is a sign of unaffordable times, she believes, and an unavoidable reality for women. Not all, of course, but many.

Pick any option: divorce, single parenthood, the inability to afford an education, limited career advancement, or a job without a company pension. Whatever the reason, too many end up with little money to show for all those decades of effort. No one tells you this in the busy years, racing out of a downtown office to pick up children from daycare, make dinner, and drive to hockey or gymnastics in time for the warmup. No raises are forthcoming in those prime working years, with none requested. So, you pay for soccer tournaments and dance recitals with a line of credit or money that could have gone to the mortgage, and it's all good, of course, because the well-being of our children is priceless.

It doesn't arrive until much later, the moment of realizing your financial precarity.

Those who came before us know all of this and more.

In her Facebook messages, Susan tells other women her number one tip for surviving on the financial edge. "Before paying for housing and food, pay for your car," she says. "Always own a car because the difference between being homeless with a car and without a car is truly day and night."

• • •

For a long time after her partner died, Pat Dunn couldn't bear to watch couples in the supermarket walk down the aisles, laughing, hands touching. "Can you grab the laundry detergent, dear," the woman might say. Or maybe he'd call out, "Hey hon, let's get steaks for dinner."

Those moments left Pat flushed with an unexpected jealousy, believing she would likely never again experience a man's hand resting on her hip in a way that made her feel wanted and safe. To her, those happy couples seemed so smug yet so familiar, from a land she once inhabited with Dave, her second partner, tall and handsome, with happy eyes like hers. As a widow in her late 60s with little money and a shrinking pool of potential partners, opportunities waned.

That yearning for connection with another person, a romance perhaps, never really leaves. Women in their 90s speak about the desire for sex, and while some rely on self-pleasure, or maybe just self-restraint, there remains a natural craving for physical intimacy, the joy of falling easily into another person's arms.

The sadness comes from the voices of others, those who tell women to give it up, they are too old, undesirable . . . unwanted.

It's all there in society, in the media, though some celebrities, like Salma Hayek, are pushing back.

Often the attractiveness of older women is rated by equally old men, in part a result of supply and demand. In 2024, Canada had 2.4 million men over the age of 70 compared to three million women; while these figures clearly indicate an early attrition rate for men, the wonderfully bodacious male ego is known to have a different interpretation. Some respond to the lopsided power in this numbers game by getting choosy. It is always confounding to see an older guy with receding hair and a waistline that holds the visceral fat of heart disease criticize a woman for her age, let alone the way she looks. Quelle audacity!

Years after Dave died, when Pat was living a step above poverty, she decided to give online dating a try. After all, that was how she'd met Dave in the early days of computer connections, a comparatively wholesome approach for a woman who had been with one man, her husband, until the age of 50. This time, she had four dates, slept with two men, and concluded that modern hookups are not for the faint of heart.

She had a lovely time with a slightly older gentleman, in his 70s, who was an intelligent conversationalist, which is important to Pat. But he told her that he does not date women near his age; he prefers them younger. "I know it's probably shallow," he told her, "but that is how I feel."

That conversation shook Pat, as if he spoke a universal truth that she had somehow missed. "I needed to hear it," she says. "I have wrinkles."

Pat is tall, five-foot-nine, with a head of ringlets that have eased from brown to silver. She's quick to smile; is smart, funny, blunt; and likes men who are thoughtful. If this sounds like a dating profile, well, it does not matter now because even though Pat wanted to find another relationship that last conversation made her give up.

She justifies her acceptance of his words by acknowledging the double whammy of grief over Dave's death and her low income, saying men want a woman who is financially able to take care of herself. (Some want women to take care of them.) It was true: Pat had little money.

Whether that man was even able to get a date with a younger woman, his words stopped her from trying again. When she describes this conversation, Pat speaks as if his beliefs are hard facts, a fait accompli.

Of course, there is always a contrarian.

In the United States, Kyrié Carpenter is the co-founder of Old School, focused on anti-ageism advocacy, created with author Ashton Applewhite and activist Ryan Backer. At the age of 38, Carpenter refers to herself a "crone-in-training," a proactive embrace of the older woman she will become. In our discussion of the ageism that Pat faced, Carpenter quickly suggested a solution. Younger men. "It's the first place my mind goes," she says, laughing.

And while an older man with a younger woman remains a more consistent scenario of an age differential, Carpenter says ideas are shifting. Not all relationships are based on the need to procreate, she points out, so the belief that the younger man with an older woman scenario is doomed due to the biological drive for children is not necessarily true. Some people do not want children. Others already have them.

"Are relationships for the purpose of intimacy between two people being met through connection and [sex]? Or are relationships for the purpose of making children?" she asks.

"In the younger man, older woman relationship, especially if we're talking post-menopause, it's not going to be for creating a family. And I think our world has really come around to see there is a huge value for partnership and intimacy outside of just procreation."

The point is to stay open to possibilities, she says. A few days after interviewing Carpenter, I received a Facebook message that appeared to be from my stalwart aunt, a widowed 85-year-old, but surely this was written with a teenage giddiness.

"He's 80 but he thinks he's 20!" she wrote of a half-decade younger dude. "I have been very happy since meeting him to say the least."

I called my cousin to ask if our aunt's Facebook account had been hacked, but it was true: She had a boyfriend. He had known her husband years earlier and initially called looking for him. Their conversation continued. He lives in the far regions of northern Ontario, an outdoorsman, invigorated by nature, it seems. One phone call led to the next, and soon a visit was planned. He drove a thousand kilometres south, arriving with a dog, a cat, and a vacuum cleaner, which I assume was meant to pick up animal hair, meaning he was not only a determined man but one who could anticipate household needs.

A few months later, I spoke with a woman whose husband had died suddenly after 50 good years of marriage. She mourned his loss, but to get out of the house, Susi Bowen joined community groups, seeking women friends although there was no shortage of men fluttering around. Susi wanted none of it until, at the age of 71, she met Rick Benson, a widower six years her junior.

As Rick tells it, he fell hard. Susi had humour and energy, a lightness, that made him want to be in her presence. And physically, he found her very attractive. On the other side of this blossoming scenario, Susi was unsure, wondering, at her age, what to expect of a relationship not to mention sex with a new man. In her mind, she imagined intercourse would be different. Maybe stodgier. Not like being a teenager and hungry for it all the time, she thought. Until the moment arrived.

"And it's exactly the same as when you're 16!" she says, laughing. "When it's right, it's right. And, you don't have to struggle with it. It's an important part of our relationship and we love it."

Late-life romance does exist. And yet it still seems impossible to forget Pat's experience with an older man's disdain of a woman near his age. I share this inequity with author and advocate Laura Tamblyn Watts. That ego, she says, is likely bolstered by the patriarchal belief that men remain dominant across the lifespan, giving some a false mirror image of themselves.

"Ageism against a person of equal years is a form of social anorexia," says Tamblyn Watts, CEO of CanAge, a national advocacy organization for older people, and author of *Let's Talk About Aging Parents*. "Women have been trained their whole lives that they need to look a certain way. They need to have beauty routines, and they need to have things that strap them down and lift them up and separate them. But that's not the message given to men for a whole bunch of reasons, including privilege and patriarchy," she says.

Internally, aging men can struggle with their new place in the world, trying to find a path forward when the pieces that previously provided external power, athleticism, business acumen, or good looks slide into decline, Tamblyn Watts says. Unable to create a new version of themselves, she believes many hold tight to their old self-image, the young virile version, to keep their sense of self intact.

"That is unhelpful for men," she says, "but it really sucks for women."

It is with curiosity then that we explore ageism among queer and lesbian women. Do they share the same values as some straight men about a potential partner's worthiness?

In short, not so much.

Yes, ageism exists everywhere, and it is hard to escape, but it may be somewhat less entrenched in the women-loving-women community. Perhaps the female ego is not as dependent on the visual or on the validation and approval some men receive from seeing others stare at their woman.

Maybe the reasons lie deeper. To be clear, I asked academics and advocates if they had seen research on this narrow topic — comparing the way straight men view older women to the way queer and lesbian women view older women — and if any such studies exist, none came to mind. There is research on aging and older lesbians, and some says that many will survive on a lower income in their later years, not to mention the challenges faced in nursing homes where same sex relationships are often condemned. But on the specific question inspired by Pat's dating experience, this next section is based not on hard data but educated observations.

Kyrié Carpenter has discussed ageism in workshops with queer people in various life stages. "What I heard first is that our world is incredibly ageist," she says. "It has expanding but narrow ideals of beauty, and we all like beautiful things. We can choose to sort of override that first impulse, but youth and beauty are appealing and queer people aren't immune to that just because they are queer.

"Everyone wants to be with the hot person, and in our current culture, a lot of times that also means the young or the younger-appearing person. What I've also witnessed in the queer community is that we're already used to bucking social norms so there's a shorter learning curve to soften that immediate bias toward beauty and toward youth. There's more receptivity when it's called out.

"Also, in the queer community, you're already working outside of the hetero procreation rules, so to speak. There's more flexibility, naturally, when it comes to age because the biological-clock conversation is different. Obviously having children in a queer relationship is already going to be more complicated than in a relationship without any fertility problems. But hey, you're already sort of operating outside of the perceived norm, which creates even more opportunity to raise your consciousness and to check your biases and to be in conversation about what is possible and what actually matters."

Dr. Ashley Flanagan, a PhD researcher with a focus on aging and the queer community, wants to make clear that she, like Carpenter, is speaking from personal observation. Flanagan believes that growing up, many queer or lesbian women were not as influenced by the visual barrage of images denoting the traditional beauty and acceptable age range that fed into society's perspective of a woman's value.

It is homosexual men, Flanagan says, who face the most ageism. "I'll make the distinction pretty clear here, when I think about queer culture, it's often a very youth-centric culture that is predominantly situated within the gay male gaze — what is desirable in terms of gay men's bodies and relationships and interactions," says Flanagan, a senior knowledge broker at the Ontario Centres for Learning, Research, and Innovation in Long-Term Care at Bruyère and an associate fellow at the National Institute on Ageing.

"However, when you step inside the queer women's community and lesbian community, there is more of a sense of community, more of a sense of relationship or relational being, which, I think, sets relationships with queer women apart from what you think about with all the stereotypes of aging and invisibility. I think within the women-loving-women communities or women-identified communities, there is much more fluidity and much more romantic attraction regardless of age."

Ashley's comments are anecdotal and yet they ring true. If young women, in general, had to survive society's expectations or judgment of their bodies, those who grew up knowing they were attracted to other women likely had other challenges to work through.

As a result, she says, women who identify as queer or lesbian are usually much more aware of the stereotypes placed on them. This has, generally, led to a different perception of a woman's worth and is less focused on what Flanagan calls the gold standard of beauty. (A standard that is ever changing.)

"I think it is a very intentional move to push back against the stereotypes, to push back against that kind of misogyny, realistically, that is deeply embedded within a certain Canadian society. So, yes, it is very intentional. It's very much, if I could go so far as to say, a reclamation of relationships and what is valued within relationships," she says. "In queer women, and it definitely applies to older women who have been on the forefront of advocacy of all the significant movements in queer rights throughout the decades, I don't think that the way that we interact, the way we love, the way we come together, happens by accident."

What about the basic question of ageism? Is there a queer woman equivalent of the man who told Pat she is too old for him, despite his own advanced years?

"I am hesitant to generalize, but I would be genuinely, genuinely shocked," she says. "I'm not saying that ageism doesn't exist in queer women communities. It certainly does. But, at a broader scale, I know many women who are in relationships with a significant age gap."

Society in general isn't terribly self-reflective about such issues and hasn't yet given deep consideration to our growing longevity and its impact on relationships. Nor are we considering whether the rise of older women — the vast numbers who are expected to remain active in the world through jobs, creative expression, or financial freedom — will mean that age discrimination lessens.

We are all impacted by the laws of timing, and Pat still feels pushed aside. She loves the company of kind men, and it cut deeply to hear that she was just too old. Pat took that man's comments to heart and for years tried to crush that part of her, the vulnerability of a woman seeking love. Eventually it went away, tucked to the side, a place she no longer ventures.

• • •

In the mid-1980s, at the age of 42, decades before anyone coined the term *grey divorce*, Elizabeth ended her marriage. In the decades since, she has lived alone, one of the 1.123 million older women who, according to Statistics Canada, do the same, paying the full cost of housing and expenses that might otherwise be shared.

Elizabeth is a pseudonym, but her life is real. Like Pat and Susan, who allowed the use of their names, I spent many hours interviewing Elizabeth, who lives in a tiny basement apartment in Toronto.

She was raised in the 1940s and 1950s to be, as she calls it, "a good girl." She earned an undergraduate degree in English literature, remained chaste until marriage, and later stayed home with two sons. When her husband had the opportunity to work overseas, she followed. When his job brought him back to Canada, she returned with him, and they bought a nice, affordable house in a southern Ontario university town. As her boys grew older, Elizabeth found work in non-profits. When her marriage fell apart, she bought her ex-spouse out of the matrimonial home, which, at the time, was not an expensive proposition.

It was a well-travelled middle-class life. For many reasons, including marginal contributions to the Canada Pension Plan and the lack of a workplace pension, it would not remain that way.

Elizabeth has many talents, but it is worth noting that, at the age of 84, she is a fast walker. So aggressively fast, it is fair to assume with only minor exaggeration that she has the VO2 max of a healthy 40-year-old, which, according to the science-based podcast bros, is a predictor of longevity. Another indicator is family history. Her mother, a woman of hardy stock, lived well past 100. Elizabeth's maternal grandparents came close.

This information is both impressive and terrifying. Elizabeth could outlive her money.

In 2025, she had $270,000 invested, her only savings left after selling her house years earlier and paying off a line of credit she used for major repairs and renovations. It was one of those nice two-storey homes with one stained-glass window and light wood trim.

Sometimes we make decisions, such as selling our house and choosing to rent, based on practicalities. That was the decision Elizabeth made 14 years ago. It was logical at the time. Outside of the HGTV-real-estate-obsessed, who was to know that the cost of houses and rentals would spiral ever upward? Timing, as they say, is a curse. The unanticipated outcome of this decision is particularly impactful on Elizabeth, clearly blessed with strong DNA. After selling her house at the age of 70, she entered a period of extraordinarily expensive living that, in her case, required enough money to survive 30 years or more. Elizabeth's savings must cover rent and food; if her health changes, there's the unpredictable costs of aging such as tens of thousands of dollars a year for private home care or for the equipment needed to navigate life in the later years. Many of us do not realize that growing old is incredibly expensive.

When her Toronto landlord said he wanted to take back the apartment she had rented in his home, Elizabeth raced, panicking, to find a new place in two months. She was happy, even thrilled, to get the tiniest of basement apartments.

Is Elizabeth poor? Not with some savings, but she needs to fund a very long life. So she lives with enforced simplicity on the strictest of budgets. Her philosophy on this unexpected turn of longevity remains steadfast. Elizabeth belongs to the silent generation, those born between 1928 and 1945, preceding the first wave of the, dare we say, more bombastic boomers.

A believer in the pull-up-your-bootstraps philosophy of life, Elizabeth manages. She has no workplace pension because she stayed at home for years and her later jobs did not offer that benefit. Elizabeth does not want to be dependent on her sons. She doesn't want them to worry even though she knows they would help if asked. Elizabeth can make do with what she's got.

It is open for debate, but at least in North America, there is no social contract that says children must support their parents when they, too, are juggling impossible mortgages and raising families. In 2023, the average cost of raising a child to the age of 17 in a two-parent household ranged from $293,000 to $400,000, according to Statistics Canada.

(One legal expert has noted that a little-known "filial responsibility" is enshrined in the Ontario Family Law Act, stating that every adult child "has an obligation to provide support, in accordance with need, for his or her parent who has cared for or provided support for the child, to the extent that the child is capable of doing so." It is unclear if any parent has acted on this.)

For now, Elizabeth lives on small monthly payments from CPP along with Old Age Security. Since she receives CPP, however limited, she does not qualify for the Guaranteed Income Supplement.

If she keeps expenses low, Elizabeth might be able to survive on her savings for the rest of her life, although they declined considerably in recent years after a series of expenses, including thousands of dollars for an oral health emergency that arrived before Canada's dental insurance plan began. If her health diminishes, Elizabeth knows how fast her money will disappear.

"It could be gone in a few years," she says.

That is what keeps Elizabeth in the basement.

• • •

It may have been the twist of timing that pushed these three women into the fiscal challenge of their older years, but however exhausting, their responses created space for new lives, carved from necessity.

Simply put, it is what they've got. And in many ways, this is where a great many older women find themselves. They managed husbands, did the domestic labour, worked outside the house, spent their money on children and sometimes buried those husbands, if not literally then emotionally. Looking back, there was no guarantee of a poetic ending. While unique in experience,

Pat, Susan, and Elizabeth are all aging on a low income in prohibitively expensive times.

Elizabeth is not destitute but ran into the crush of unaffordable housing and is deeply aware that her expected arrival in the centenarian club means she could outlast her money.

Pat had a plan, and a good man, but ended up alone with little money in her late 60s. It led to a reckoning on finances, yes, but also her desire for intimacy, a feeling she has since locked away. Now, she relies on an internal narrative that says had her partner lived, she would have never encountered the callousness of some men. She would still be in love and making love, a desire shared by many. Pat sought a new purpose. True to the observation that necessity breeds invention, she created a novel path forward not just for herself but for others, and today she helps financially struggling women find roommates through her nonprofit, Senior Women Living Together.

Susan, well, she knows how it feels to live in a car, which is a lot better than living on the street. She also got lucky. In 2004, a friend of hers, who clearly excels in long-term thinking, put her name on a wait-list for social housing, and 18 years later, Susan got the call. She can just afford to pay rent in a building attached to an Ottawa church that is home, she says, to a bunch of old progressive '70s hippies. While she fears this blessing will one day be sold off for condos, Susan also can't bear the thought of staring at its four walls for the remainder of her days. She spends part of the year on the road when she feels well enough, though, as she feared, her health is not shifting in her favour.

It may be comforting to try, but let's not differentiate ourselves, not too much, from these three women. In their own ways, they represent the unexpected twists of life that come for many of us. The harsh times, yes, but also the fresh starts, created by ingenuity.

Their stories expose the loneliness from a catastrophic loss, the enduring gender pension gap, and the crushing cost of housing in harsh economic times. But they also speak of resilience and renewal.

These are the astonishing lives of older women.

RETIREMENT BENEFIT FACTS

Canada Pension Plan and Quebec Pension Plan: We make contributions during our working lives to CPP or QPP, from the age of 18 until retirement—roughly 40 years. The *maximum* monthly CPP payment starting at the age of 65 was $1,433 in 2025 for a total of $17,196 a year. The *average* CPP monthly payment in 2025 was $808.14 or $9,607.68 a year. The average woman gets less.

Old Age Security: Depending on income and marital status, the maximum OAS in the second quarter of 2025 for those aged 65 to 74 was roughly $730 per month. For those aged 75 and older, it was just over $800. To qualify, you must live in Canada for at least a decade after the age of 18.

Guaranteed Income Supplement: As of March 2025, if you were 65 plus and single, widowed, or divorced with an income below $22,056, you were eligible for a GIS payment that maxes out at $1,086.88. But don't count on it. For every dollar of income earned—above a grace amount—GIS is reduced by 50 percent, leaving many with next to nothing.

CHAPTER TWO

The CEO

For most of us, the word *longevity* symbolizes lifespan and well-being.

Podcast hosts with PhDs record hours of audio on the benefits of time-restricted eating, resveratrol supplements, or the impact of vegetables on the gut-brain axis, all focused on the potential of a long and healthy existence.

Leanne Kaufman believes financial longevity is an equally compelling conversation. Not just for the many older women who are struggling on a low income but also for a younger generation that may not consider the impact of their current career decisions decades later.

As president and CEO of RBC Royal Trust, Kaufman, a lawyer by training, has spent years building partnerships with organizations that focus on the aging experience, offering legal and financial expertise to elevate public awareness on the need to prepare for the unexpected.

It is fair to say that many of us believe we will grow old without losing our power. If we are physically and cognitively strong in our 40s or 60s, we assume it will be ever thus, though we acknowledge the value of exercise and nutrition. However, the later-in-life manifestation of diseases such as cancer or Alzheimer's can leave us unprepared and incapacitated, unable to properly make sound choices and legal decisions for ourselves.

No matter what the future holds, there is immeasurable value in teaching Canadians that the best defence against the unknown is found in estate and capacity planning, including the designation of at least one power of attorney to manage your money if the day comes when you cannot.

Kaufman's public-service partnerships began in 2020 with the National Institute on Ageing, a think tank at Toronto Metropolitan University where, as an advisory board member, she offers expertise on financial literacy used in research and awareness campaigns for older adults.

She soon established another partnership, with Women's Age Lab at Women's College Hospital, founded by geriatrician and senior scientist Dr. Paula Rochon, to raise awareness on gendered ageism. The Women's Age Lab aims to eliminate medical research bias against women while also focusing on the gender pension gap, the impact of loneliness, and the need for housing innovation to help Canadians age in the right place. As RBC Wealth Management has said of this partnership, the "combination of sexism and ageism is a major barrier to healthy aging for older women. Together, we want to break down this barrier and improve health, social and financial well-being for senior women."

It was through Dr. Rochon that Kaufman learned of the gender pension gap, a measurement that explains so much even though society discusses it so rarely. "When you hear some of the stats or some of the points that they're bringing to light, of course it makes perfect sense," Kaufman says. "But I hadn't thought about it before, and if I hadn't thought about it before and I work in the financial services industry, I imagine a lot of other people haven't thought of it."

The gender pension gap, she says, shows that financial planning for women is not the same as it is for men. And since she works in a sector where clients have at least some assets to invest and later disburse, Kaufman began exploring the financial challenges of aging while female, recognizing that women with decent salaries also experience a gap in retirement income compared to their male colleagues. It is an equal opportunity inequity, and for some, the impact is severe.

"A lot of financial planning hasn't been designed specifically for women historically," she says. "Drawing an analogy to the medical field, we know that Alzheimer's shows up differently in women than it does in men, and heart disease can show up differently in women. And the research is always done on the men. This is sort of a natural extension of another example of these truly female gender specific roles and paradigms that just haven't caught up with the traditional sense of what we think about when we talk financial planning and, by extension, estate planning and capacity planning."

While some men are starting to take parental leave, their contribution to raising children, however worthy, is often shorter than women's. As such, the difference in the female employment experience continues, she says. Many women fall behind in workplace pension investment, unless there is an affordable option to "buy back" missed payments. Years later, it is usually the women, Kaufman notes, who take time off work again to be caregivers for aging parents or an ailing spouse.

"We know everybody is working longer into retirement than we historically have," Kaufman says. "Women tend to outlive their partners, and there may be caregiving requirements there. And so, all of those are times when it's more likely that a woman rather than a man will wind up stepping away or stepping out of the workforce and earning an income at these critical life event moments."

In later years, she says, a new financial pain can emerge after a spouse's death. And as we know, it is often the women who end up alone. Some inherit the full share of the bills. Others benefit from a survivor's pension, however reduced. While it is true that women are increasingly employed in public sector jobs with good pensions, leading to a recent uptick in pensions, it is also worth acknowledging that compared to 50 years ago, the overall number of Canadians with a workplace pension is in decline.

"When you're talking about late-life planning, women again probably outlive their partners, but their expenses may not drop significantly," Kaufman says. "And if they're down to a single income and it's lower than what their male partner was bringing in, that's where I think they feel the gap, again in those late-life stages."

Kaufman hosts an RBC Royal Trust podcast called *Matters Beyond Wealth*, discussing estate planning, healthy aging, and finances for the future, including retirement. The topics are diverse but the goal, she says, is education. What is heartening, she adds, is that public engagement with the podcast shows an interest in learning how to plan for a long life. But it is especially important for women in the early stages of a career to learn the value of long-term planning, she says.

"I think this particular topic really lends itself to the younger generation or the next generation because so much of the prevention, if there's any prevention to be done, needs to be done before you're 65 and ready to retire, or whenever you are ready to retire."

So, from the CEO of RBC Royal Trust, here is straight talk on preparing for a long life.

The Earlier Years

While the financial impact of parental leave likely won't change a woman's decision to take what is clearly important time with her baby (and recovery from a pregnancy), it is also true that for every parental leave a woman takes, the value of her private workplace pension will diminish. Talk to a financial planner, Kaufman says, to understand your specific needs moving forward, and find out if there is a buy-back option that allows you to replace missed pension payments once you're back to work — if you can afford to do so.

An education in pensions would go a long way to help younger people make better job choices. Although many companies do not offer these retirement benefits, there is a significant difference between a defined benefit pension, which provides payments for life, and a defined contribution plan, which is similar to a personal investment account. There are other forward-thinking options, Kaufman says, such as an employee shared purchase plan, which allows workers to buy shares in a company through regular paycheque deductions or lump-sum payments.

"A small amount early in your career can make a big difference to you at the end of your career and in your late life," says Kaufman.

The Middle Years

For some perspective on the urgent need to get your legal documents in order, here are a few illuminating points.

Compared to men, women are more likely to develop Alzheimer's disease or other forms of cognitive decline and are more than twice as likely to die from Alzheimer's disease.

With the exception of early onset dementia, the prevalence of dementia roughly doubles every five years after the age of 65. While Statistics Canada notes some decline in dementia, potentially attributed to the way doctors register causes of death, current numbers show that after the age of 85, one in four is likely to be diagnosed with the disease. And in 20 years, the number of Canadians aged 85 and older could triple to 2.5 million. The majority will be women.

Each individual's trajectory with Alzheimer's is unique, but after what can be a long period of significant decline, most no longer have the capacity, or cognitive ability, to make financial decisions.

As Kaufman says, it's best to get estate and capacity planning done early, designating trusted family, friends, or a professional to manage health and finances, should the need arise. "Have you made a substitute decision maker? Have you created a power of attorney document, and how are you going to fund that portion of your life, even if you're not as cognitively aware of what's going on as you would like to be?"

Listening to podcasts focused on longevity, especially those hosted by physicians, such as Dr. Peter Attia (author of *Outlive*), I notice there seems to be growing evidence that cardio exercise and strength building may contribute to a healthier and longer life. The demographic shift toward longevity led to

Kaufman's work with the AgeLab at the Massachusetts Institute of Technology in Cambridge, Massachusetts. It has a growing focus on the need for a well-considered retirement plan since our extra decades are rerouting the more traditional trajectory of golf, sunshine, and death.

"Retirement planning today isn't just planning for the first five or ten years after you stop working when you're all about travel and pickleball and playing in the backyard with your grandkids. We have to think about the full life cycle," she says.

Despite a growing interest among older Canadians, many are not getting the work of retirement planning done. According to research by RBC Royal Trust and the National Institute on Ageing, only 48 percent of Canadians have a will setting out plans for asset disbursal and just 35 percent have appointed a power of attorney.

The implications vary across provinces, and without delving into all the legal nuances, it is fair to say that unless our affairs are in order, the efforts of family or caregivers will be considerably slowed. A missing will could require a lengthy search for information on assets; without a legally designated power of attorney, an expensive court hearing may be needed to request the creation and control of a management plan for the incapacitated individual.

"It leaves a big mess for the family or friends left behind," Kaufman says, "but it also puts the incapable person in this state of limbo where there might be a period of time where really no one has the authority to deal with their assets, which obviously can come with great challenges."

The blessing of longevity requires paperwork. Listen to the expert and get it done, while you can.

CHAPTER THREE

Pat

In the beginning, it was love.

This is not the story of Pat's first husband, whom she divorced in 2000 at the age of 50, after the children had mostly left home. He let it be known with precise words that the marriage had ended, perhaps, she later mused, because she was studying part-time for a degree in nursing and he absorbed more child-rearing duties of teenagers.

"I do not love you anymore," he said. It was honest.

Life doesn't always present us with the most compatible partner the first or even second time around. For Pat, it seemed equal parts sad and natural, the ending of a 30-year-marriage to a man she very much liked but didn't necessarily love, not in that head-over-heels way that she wanted to experience at least once.

To understand the joy of Pat's later-in-life love, let's begin with her marriage.

She was a tall and skinny 21-year-old with dreams of a traditional family but prepared for the future with a nursing diploma when she married in 1972. Pat was a kid really, and their first child, a daughter, arrived two years later. Pat found her husband's humour captivating, sardonic, and so quick that she knew he had a good mind; still, theirs was never the romance that she read about in historical novels with leading female characters who were strong-willed yet swooned in the embrace of a charming man.

They lived in Oakville, where Pat had spent her teenage years, and then moved to a little village south of Barrie, buying a big brick home with a swimming pool. Later, when small town life became, well, too small for Pat, they bought a house in a middle-class suburb in Oakville's west end.

As it does, life took its toll. Pat's second child, a sweet ten-pound, three-ounce boy born in 1975, was diagnosed with congenital heart disease. Baby Paul was in and out of hospitals for years, enjoying every scoop of ice cream that came his way, waiting until doctors felt he had the strength to manage heart surgery. It took five years before surgeons scheduled his operation. All indications showed it went well. Paul died the next day. Pat's eyes normally shine, but when she speaks of his death, they are dull.

Two years after Paul died, they adopted a toddler, another boy, who was born with significant intellectual delays. Her husband worked hard during those years, first as an electrician, then with his business, and later as vice-president of an up-and-coming company focused on electrical contracting. It was the 1980s. Construction was booming. They soon added a 32-foot sailboat to the mix, purchased with cash from her husband's unexpected work bonus and, naming it *Windfall*, they joined the Bronte Harbour Yacht Club. It completed the vision of respectable suburbia.

The death of a child can destroy a marriage, and as Pat watched her daughter grieve the loss of Paul, her little brother, she made the decision to stay close to her husband. Not just for herself but her daughter too. For a long time, it worked. Cooking dinners, weekends on the *Windfall*, and taking care of the family, she kept the house running while her husband worked his way up the corporate ladder. And yet, somewhere along the way, Pat lost interest in her marriage. She wanted to get a university degree in nursing, an improvement on her original training in a hospital, and juggling part-time studies with home life, Pat earned a degree at McMaster University. It opened her eyes to new ideas, a career in public health, and as her husband handled a greater share of child care responsibilities, Pat grew curious, seeking more from life, planning trips that seemed unimaginable a few years earlier. She spoke of home-sharing in Australia or South America. Her husband was not interested. They got caught in the drift, the way many couples silently part, creating lives away from each other, until somebody has an affair or says the words "I do not love you anymore."

Even though it made sense, Pat greeted the dissolution of her marriage as an existential threat. She'd clench the steering wheel of her car while stopped at a red light and wonder, "Who am I if I am not married?" And yet she had already started creating a new, independent life as a public health nurse, a job she would hold for 14 years but that ultimately would not be enough for a substantial monthly payment from CPP or a lucrative government pension.

In March 2000, long before she quit her nursing job, Pat was diagnosed with possible thyroid cancer. She had surgery in June. Two days later, doctors found a pulmonary embolism, blood clots, in her lungs. As it turned out, it wasn't cancer. In September, with the marriage officially over, the family home went on the market.

In the early 2000s, no one imagined that housing would one day become unattainably expensive. And so, after paying off real estate and legal fees, not to mention the line of credit for a new car and all the costs of maintaining a healthy Oakville life, Pat said she and her ex-husband each departed their marriage with $50,000, plus some money in RRSPs. As part of the divorce settlement, he had to pay her alimony for a few years. At the age of 50, on her own for the first time since she was that skinny 21-year-old, Pat put her $50,000 into a high interest savings account.

It was no longer the life of a yacht-club couple, but it was a fresh start, and Pat took six weeks off work to volunteer in Peru with impoverished older people living in the mountains. They all shared a home and, she discovered, shoes. One person wore the pair of shoes on Monday, the next person got the shoes on Tuesday, and so on. Their poverty was startling to her. The experience shook her out of a reverie of sorts, normalizing this new life as a single woman. Even for those who crave change, who go on to thrive, endings can lead to introspection.

Like most public health nurses whose purses seem to hold untold necessities like packages of dental floss or condoms for teenagers, Pat's always had a notebook and pen. On the flight home from Peru, she dug them out of her bag, unfolded the seat tray, and, staring down at the blank page, wrote the words "Conditions of Satisfaction for My Future."

It was intended as an exercise to examine the wide expanse of opportunities for her new life, but in that moment, soaring above the clouds, surrounded by strangers, her focus narrowed. To men. Pat liked men. Specifically, she liked intelligent men, the very best kind.

Yes, she still believed in the 1960s feminism that told women they did not need a husband. And she had been impressionable in the 1970s when 20-something women wore T-shirts that read "A woman needs a man like a fish needs a bicycle." The message of independence, of self-reliance, was clear, and for Pat, it resonated all these years later. She knew she could live without a man, and yet, contemplating that blank notebook page, her interior voice said, "But I don't want to."

And so began the list of conditions for satisfaction in a future partner.

At five-foot-nine, Pat wanted a man who was taller. He had to be funny, she wrote. Kind. Have a sense of adventure. Willing to spend on experiences instead of possessions. And proving that women can also be sticklers for looks, she wrote the physical traits of her ideal guy. Slim. Physically fit. And attractive to her, because while a good face is relative, it matters.

She arrived home to the culture shock of abundance, from the grocery store aisles loaded with inestimable options for food, particularly the jars of peanut butter that she had craved while away. In her condo, groceries placed in cupboards, she emptied her purse and pulled out the notebook. Reading her list of conditions, Pat wondered, "How am I going to meet this man?"

She wasn't going to meet him at work, since most of her colleagues were women and dating male clients wasn't going to happen, so she emailed friends to let them know she was open to introductions and joined a dating site (Pat has long forgotten which one). She was pleased to see that after posting her profile, sans photo, messages arrived.

One man seemed entertaining over the phone, but in emails, she did not like his sentence structure. Grammar matters. Another reached out under the name Tackman, which Pat thought could be a reference to sailing, an intriguing quality since her profile said she was a boater. Tackman's real name was David. She agreed to meet him outside the Montana's restaurant in Burlington, which was probably not the most romantic setting given its high-demand children's menu.

On date night, in her little condo, Pat stared at herself in the mirror. She needed a good hair day. Pulling out her hair dryer, she started rolling her hair with a brush, blowing out the curls until she finished with a thick mass of waves that would, no doubt, grow bigger as the evening progressed.

She put on pants and a sweater, admiring the profile of her 50-year-old self. With a sweep of mascara and blush on her cheeks, Pat was ready to go. Nervous could not begin to describe how she felt, but mostly she was excited. "This is the start of your adventure," she told herself. Pat didn't want to feel superficial, but she was following her conditions for a man, after all, and she wondered if his looks would match the words she wrote on the airplane.

Her legs felt a bit shaky as she walked toward the restaurant, allowing families rushing for a table to pass. As the crowd disappeared inside the front doors, she saw a man turn. He was tall. Slim. Dark hair. A good face. He watched her walk toward him, and he smiled. She didn't know what to do, so she laughed. Though this was long before Instagram influencers brought the ancient concept of manifestation to their followers, in that moment, Pat believed that her written list of conditions had presented her with this lovely man.

Inside Montana's, she ordered wine, he got a beer. They talked for hours about life, children, marriage, dreams, travel. When Pat's questions about his marriage hit a nerve, he said, "I don't want to talk about that now." He seemed patient, gentle. She wanted to see him again.

At her car, it became clear that he felt the same way. He turned Pat around to face him and leaned down to kiss her in the softest of ways — except they didn't stop and when a carload of teenagers drove past, one rolled down the window and shouted,

"Get a room!" Pat and David laughed. It all felt like magic. They continued kissing inside her car, getting to know each other somewhat more intimately until she stopped him and said, "I have to go; my son is at home." He said, "Don't you want to come before you go?" which may have been one of the corniest lines ever spoken on a first date, but to Pat, it felt like fire. She went home that night wondering how an orgasm would feel, because at the age of 50, she still did not know, not really, at least not in an omigod kind of way. How do you know what you don't know?

After that first night, Pat and Dave, as she called him, started meeting for dinner. They went for walks. They talked over wine. "Ah," she thought, "so this is dating." Their conversations carried on for hours. He loved reading, and one night she saw a book on his coffee table, she can't recall the name, except that it was nonfiction and sounded fascinating. They talked about its thesis. It made her brain feel alive. He spoke about his philosophy of child-rearing, his belief in raising a daughter who would walk into the world with strength, knowing her power. It was an intellectual stimulation that she had never before experienced. She watched the way Dave moved, the elegance of his body; she saw the way his eyes followed her. It felt like she was on top of a mountain, out of breath. Six months after their first date, Pat and Dave moved in together.

It always seems magnetic when two people feel that spark for each other. Not to ruin the moment or centuries of poetry written about its elusiveness, but falling in love, according to science, is the alchemy of hormones and brain chemicals; the mutual explosion of dopamine, serotonin, and oxytocin between two people is a beautiful thing. Pat had never felt it until she and Dave fell in love.

It would last for the rest of his life.

CHAPTER FOUR

Elizabeth

Elizabeth lives in the basement of an old house known for its past life as a Buddhist centre. It is now broken into apartments, and Elizabeth's one room plus a washroom is the tiniest. It is home.

Winter light flows through the narrow window, offering a ground-level glimpse of a laneway fence. Elizabeth lives alone. After divorcing her husband in her early 40s and a relationship with a man who seemed charming but was not, Elizabeth pledged her life to herself, family, and friends.

In her home and her philosophy, Elizabeth has built herself a little fortress against the world, including the loneliness and isolation that harm others. It's part of her strategy on financing longevity, the belief that one need not spend a lot of money to be socially connected.

Admittedly, it is hard to start over in the later years. Hard to connect, as a single woman, with couples who have been friends, seemingly forever and have their world settled, politely avoiding the odd woman out. But there are ways.

For Elizabeth, the shyness she felt as a young mother, moving with her husband from his job overseas back to Ontario, is no different than the reticence she feels now when approaching new people. What she figured out decades ago, as a lonely mom with a stroller walking the sidewalks and wishing for adult conversation, is that others feel the same, so trust yourself to find them. Back then, she scoped out homes with a baby carriage on the front porch and, heart beating, knocked on the front door, introducing herself. The women who answered became her friends for the next 30 years.

What this experience taught Elizabeth is the value of ingenuity, a bit of forced toughness along with the stoicism that emerged from the ancient writings of the Roman emperor-philosopher Marcus Aurelius whose meditations would one day find a rapt audience on TikTok, although that is not Elizabeth's vibe. Hard-core resilience is best summoned sparingly, in the worst of times. It can be exhausting to start anew, but Elizabeth is not a complainer.

Music is her friend. Elizabeth prefers wind instruments. She still plays in a band, and while that costs a bit of money, it's worth every penny. Research tells us that people who live with a dog are among the happiest, and in Elizabeth's case, her handsome canine is a sturdy mixed breed she met at a Toronto animal shelter. He is aloof, and yet when he sits at the far end of her futon, his eyes follow Elizabeth as she takes her teacup to the kitchen sink; it is only five steps away. They live in sympatico quietly or with bursts of energy, given that Elizabeth and her good boy are vigorous walkers.

Elizabeth's relationship with her dog took her to a nearby park, a daily gathering place. It was with a dog-walking group that her fresh start began. She met a chatty guy who told her about the gang of people who leave the leash-free park at 10:30

every morning for a walk through the forest. "Why don't you join us?" he asked.

Elizabeth liked that idea, but it also scared her. All those new people. She felt shy, and for a while, she avoided the invitation, telling herself, "Oh, they don't know me, and they won't like me." Then she remembered the lonely mom version of herself, looking for homes with baby carriages in her neighbourhood. And so, when he invited her again, she showed up the next day.

The walking group has a writer, an actor, and academics. They start near the parking lot and set out down hills, through the forest, talking and laughing, a morning routine that sustains Elizabeth.

Often, our friendships are created by vicinity. Elizabeth's building, once home to Buddhists, apparently retained such a communal spirit that residents pooled their money and bought a barbecue, meeting outside not for meditation but for conversation over an occasional meal.

While not everyone can get a rescue dog or find an apartment with good neighbours, the point is Elizabeth took risks that led to friendship at a front-yard picnic table and walking in nature with those who engage in the fine art of conviviality.

Sometimes, by mustering just enough bravery, good stuff comes along.

EXPERIENTIAL DEFINITIONS

- **Social loneliness** is the perception that a desired social network does not exist.
- **Emotional loneliness** is a deep pain from the loss of a partner, relative, or confidante.
- **Existential loneliness** is the feeling of isolation stemming from, perhaps, a traumatic experience, a disease, or issues that others may not understand.
- **Social isolation** is an objective lack of meaningful connections.

CHAPTER FIVE

A Few Good Girlfriends

On her podcast *Wiser Than Me*, Julia Louis-Dreyfus, the actor and comedian who earned eternal fame as Elaine on *Seinfeld*, interviews older women about life, relationships, careers, and sex. After each interview, she calls her mother to tell her all about it. To me, it's the quintessential female experience to phone your mom after something exciting happens, and listening to this part of the podcast always makes me miss mine. She would have had thoughts on the first *Wiser Than Me* episode with 85-year-old Jane Fonda who, given her previous interviews on the incredible value of female friendship, offered a counterintuitive insight.

Fonda told Louis-Dreyfus that in her younger years, she only spent time with men, preferably the alphas. "And I had no women friends," she said. "It wasn't until I gave birth to a daughter that I started very tentatively having women friends. And then when I became an activist, it was the women that I met here in this country, the women activists, that were the most responsible for my new consciousness and transformation. Being with them was like looking at the world, looking through a keyhole at the world that we're trying to create.

"They behave like what we should all behave like, with kindness and generosity and humanity. And oh my gosh, I thought, isn't that interesting? Men have never treated me this way before. These women, there are, you know, three or four that, specifically, when they looked at me, I knew they were looking at me, not the celebrity. And I felt seen. And they asked me how I felt and what I thought about things. Men never did that."

Fonda is certainly not alone in her early focus on men, and for those who had a similar approach, it soon becomes obvious that time spent with women friends is enriching in ways that the alpha guys, even those who are charming, cannot deliver. Women have a knowing. We share hidden parts of ourselves with our most trusted female friends, and they understand. Often, they enlighten. You only need a few.

Years ago, in a studio set up for a TEDWomen Talk, Fonda sat on a dark green loveseat with her long-time friend, the actor, writer, and comedian, Lily Tomlin for an interview with U.S. media executive Pat Mitchell. Tomlin and Fonda met a few years before they starred together in the 1980 film *9 to 5*. The TEDWomen event was billed as a discussion on female friendship.

"I exist because I have my female friends," said Fonda. "They make me stronger, they make me smarter, they make me braver. They tap me on the shoulder when I might be in need of course-correcting."

There was a moment in this conversation when Fonda expressed empathy for men, saying they are mystified by female friendships because from a young age, the patriarchal culture forbids male vulnerability. "Which I think may be why they die earlier," she said.

The audience laughed, but from her expression it didn't appear Fonda was aiming for a quick joke. In any case, she is correct because in addition to the many reasons why men die earlier, data shows that men, especially much older men, have a high rate of suicide. In Ontario, the Office of the Chief Coroner says the suicide rate of men aged 80 and older is almost equal to that of younger men, traditionally considered more prone to extreme measures and who have access to the guns or ropes that ensure the effort is fatal. It is also six times higher than the suicide rates of 80-something women, though that could be due to the more definitive ways men choose to end their lives. Among the older men I interviewed for my *Toronto Star* podcast episode on that topic, one of the greatest threats is social isolation. As a widower explained, he had one male friend and they spoke by email once a year.

Paraphrasing Gloria Steinem, Fonda went on to say that women are not better than men, but in a society dominated by patriarchy, women can show vulnerability with each other, unlike men, who have to prove their masculinity. Tomlin quickly countered. Men, she said, are so comfortable with power that change will require a much different approach. Neither had a quick answer for the eternal question of patriarchy, and in any case, the conversation was focused on women, so they returned to the topic at hand.

"Women's friendships," said Fonda, "are a renewable source of power."

Whether they are celebrities in Hollywood or two retirees in Oshawa, Ontario, planning a notable arrival to the octogenarian decade, everyone needs a ride-or-die friend. For Mary Kelcey, that friend is Lina Katzman. If Mary wants to celebrate by jumping out of an airplane at 10,000 feet, Lina will jump with her.

Skydiving for newcomers, at least in southern Ontario, is a tandem experience, meaning that each woman is strapped to the front of a jumpmaster, a dude with a parachute strapped on his back, which, after 40 seconds hurtling downward at 200 kilometres an hour, blasts open for a graceful descent to a pasture below. Mary seemed pleased to be attached to a muscular skydiving instructor, whom she later described as a "strap-on hottie" to her husband, a patient man.

The adventures of Mary and Lina, documented in the *Toronto Star*, are not intended to suggest that the only way to enjoy our later years is to jump out of airplanes, ride camels, or hang off the edge of the CN Tower, officially sanctioned of course. What they do illustrate is the fun to be had in the company of a good friend. (Of course, it helps to have the disposable income to afford such events.) For many women, these friendships are a joy, even if most meet-ups are rather simpler, over lattes or morning walks.

Still, research shows that loneliness and social isolation are on the rise globally. It is a phenomenon with an intergenerational connection. Aloneness has a profound impact on people in their teens and 20s, perhaps after changing social networks in a new city for school or work, and on older people, those who have lost dear friends and partners over the years or aren't tapped into a community.

Loneliness and isolation are scary.

These conditions hurt emotionally, but physically they bring a risk of dementia, in part due to our withdrawal from society. Dementia, an umbrella term for many types of cognitive decline, is not to be taken lightly. Neither is heart disease, inflammation, or the overall debilitating decline in body and spirit that can potentially come from life with few social interactions.

One woman I interviewed, who didn't want her name used, ended up living in a tiny apartment, the cheapest she could find, near a highway noisy with truckers' air horns and late-night drag races. She had separated from her partner a few years earlier, and after moving home following decades spent in western Canada, she tried to replicate the social scene that she once had with her husband. It didn't work. She was an introvert. It was too hard, too draining, to meet up with strangers, so she retreated. She tried to organize walks with girlfriends from childhood, but they wanted to meet for lunch and she couldn't afford restaurant meals. Instead, she sat inside that apartment overlooking the highway. "I am so very, very lonely," she said. When we spoke again a year later, her voice sounded tiny, empty.

Loneliness and isolation are now on the list of public health threats for people of all ages, not just older adults, even for those busy with family and careers.

In 2023, U.S. Surgeon General Dr. Vivek H. Murthy made it his mission to discuss the recognition that for many, life hurts. In the introduction to a report, a call for action suitably named *Our Epidemic of Loneliness and Isolation*, Murthy wrote it was during a cross-country listening tour a few years earlier that he discovered the extent of Americans' aloneness:

> People began to tell me they felt isolated, invisible, and insignificant. Even when they couldn't put their finger on the word "lonely," time and time again, people of all ages and socioeconomic backgrounds, from every corner of the country, would tell me, "I have to shoulder all of life's burdens by

> myself," or "if I disappear tomorrow, no one will even notice."
>
> It was a lightbulb moment for me: social disconnection was far more common than I had realized. In the scientific literature, I found confirmation of what I was hearing. In recent years, about one-in-two adults in America reported experiencing loneliness. And that was before the COVID-19 pandemic cut off so many of us from friends, loved ones, and support systems, exacerbating loneliness and isolation.

Public health experts have recognized the plague of loneliness and social isolation spreading across the globe. In 2024, the World Health Organization created the WHO Commission on Social Connection. Its three-year mandate "aims to see the issue recognised and resourced as a global public health priority." According to WHO statistics, more than 25 percent of older adults worldwide experience social isolation and 17 percent of people in their 20s live with loneliness.

The prevalence of these conditions has awakened many physicians to the depths of this public health crisis. I once did a ride-a-long with a doctor who did at-home visits for housebound patients in downtown Toronto. As we drove along Yonge Street, she looked up at the apartment windows and said, "I wonder how many older people are in there completely alone."

It is true that many disappear into their apartments, especially as fragility sets in, spending years mostly alone unless an observant neighbour notices that something is amiss. Some of us will die alone, too, our bodies only discovered when the scent of death slips under the door.

Others grow so lonely, they are easy pickings for financial abuse, spawning the phenomenon of predatory marriage. We will do anything to shed the terrible feelings of aloneness, even sign over control of our estate to someone we hope will stick around until the end. In many cases, by handing over financial power of attorney, the money disappears.

Among people of all ages, isolation and loneliness can cause depression or suicide. Humans are social beings. We need to feel like we belong, that we matter, and for some, often younger adults, marginalization can lead to extremist views. A spate of articles in *Time*, *Newsweek*, and on CNN's website cited a 2021 study by the RAND Corporation that found the overwhelming aloneness and lack of connection to community was present in 16 of 32 individuals known to have joined extremist movements in the United States. There were other issues at play, such as financial vulnerability and mental health, but loneliness hit hard.

Membership in extremist groups undoubtedly lands on the far end of the continuum, but it is clear that social isolation and loneliness are linked to depression, which costs the global economy $1 trillion each year.

Recognition of the problem alone is not enough. The United Kingdom created a Ministry of Loneliness, funding research and boots-on-the-ground attempts at solutions. Despite international headlines, studies found it made no real improvement.

In Canada, before the long isolation of COVID harmed our collective psyche, older adults were already on a startling emotional decline. Nearly one in five aged 65 and older reported feeling lonely in 2019 and 2020, with those who never married, or were widowed, separated, or divorced more than twice as likely to report this intense aloneness. Those who fared the worst among the older cohort were women, immigrants, and people living on a low income.

Since women live longer, and often alone, let us not forget the centenarians. Longevity offers much to consider.

When I take my grand puppy outside in the early morning, I see the same two women, both in their 70s or 80s, walking and talking. Though I'm not sure what they're discussing, their conversations always seem happily intense. It is a daily routine. Maybe it's the brain of a journalist, but I sometimes wonder what would happen if one woman grew ill or died. How would her friend ever replace a connection so lovely?

While there can be great joy in a long life, it is so much better when you have companions. And, listening to the wisdom of those who come before us, it helps to find a younger friend or two, to manage the inevitable attrition.

If those women will follow you out of an airplane, it will create an unforgettable bond but, in the grand scheme, there's nothing better than the simple moments. A few good girlfriends, they're all we need.

PENSION AND RRSP FACTS

Defined Benefit Plan: The most reliable workplace pension, it is built on years of employer and employee contributions. After retirement, it pays a monthly benefit until death.

Defined Contribution Plan: More akin to an investment vehicle, its value is linked to the markets and might run out before you do.

Registered Retirement Savings Plan: An RRSP offers a tax deduction based on annual contributions. At the age of 71, it must be converted into a registered retirement income fund (RRIF) or an annuity, which provides a steady income.

CHAPTER SIX

The Millennial

At the age of 34, Stephanie Hinds is preparing for dotage. Nothing that steals from the pleasures of now: dancing at the Carnival in Trinidad, dinners with friends, and time spent with her eight-year-old daughter. It is possible to live with short- and long-term plans. Stephanie is focused on building the personal wealth that will support her as an old woman, from a good salary, savings, and a hearty pension.

Men come and go, she says, but money, well now, that can last a lifetime. Money pays for stability. Peace. A home of one's own. What's the value of longevity, Stephanie asks, if it is crushed by the stress of paying bills?

As a columnist for the popular celebrity website Lainey Gossip, writing about matrescence, money, and men, Stephanie has created a conversation for other young women about motherhood, healthy relationships, and financial independence.

And like most inspiration, her long-term plan comes from a personal place. She watched her mother prepare for retirement without a company pension, fear in her eyes, even with a husband to help. She saw how hard it was for her to leave a full-time job she didn't like for a future that could be worse.

Stephanie considered her own career trajectory and realized that she had to focus on her financial well-being. In her 20s, Stephanie used her university degree to work as a television journalist. The live feed appreciated her smart, articulate delivery, but the freelance gig offered no pension, no benefits, no paid maternity leave. Three months after her daughter was born, she was back, covering the Saturday night shift for Bell Media, just to make sure the producers didn't forget the hard-working and ambitious Stephanie Hinds.

After exchanging the allure of broadcasting for the practicality of full-time employment, Stephanie discovered that she, a young Black woman skilled at social media marketing, earned less than her colleagues. Same age. Same experience. And, despite asking, no raise was forthcoming.

Did she want to make a dramatic table-tossing exit à la *Real Housewives* that she would later analyze for Lainey Gossip? Yes, but that was not her style, not with a daughter to support. Any satisfaction she could have derived from walking out the heavy front doors of that charitable foundation shifted to a more professional response, otherwise known as revenge on ice. It's always best to leave with new employment and a glow-up salary.

So, Stephanie quietly went about finding herself a better job, and in early 2024, she got hired by a high-profile government agency. Her annual salary increased by more than $20,000. With her freelance income from Lainey Gossip, she now earns well over six figures. While that does not go nearly as far as it once did, public service jobs come with considerable benefits and the holy grail (if you pay into it long enough) of a defined benefit pension that lasts a lifetime.

Professionally, she landed in a good place with a job reflecting her worth. But the challenge of getting there taught her a lesson. All employees, she concluded, are considered disposable. While an employer may lament the loss of a worker's skill, someone else can always do the trick.

Stephanie's growing belief in personal value wasn't limited to her professional life. When her relationship with the father of her daughter became, in her view, unworkable, she ended it. Now she lives on her own, north of Toronto, in a rented townhouse with her daughter, a cat, and the serenity of personal space.

Before dawn, she sips lemon tea at her living-room desk and writes about finances, the gender pension gap, the gender wage gap, and a new topic among some young women called the Great Divorce.

In her writing, Stephanie uses celebrity news to explore finances or life choices, offering insight that a great many older women may wish they had decades earlier when the idea of retirement seemed light years away.

Schools don't generally educate students on the gender pension gap, an international problem that in Scotland led to a public awareness campaign telling young women that a typical 25-year-old will retire with £100,000 ($170,000) less than her average male peer.

Information is power.

Whether married with children or embarking on the Great Divorce, financial knowledge matters, particularly when making the decision to navigate life alone. Society seems most comfortable with those who embrace the continuity of a job or long-time partner, but as Stephanie writes, a woman doesn't need to accept a less-than-wonderful relationship with a man. Nor must she meekly accept a salary that does not represent her contribution.

To her, these are fear-based commitments that are more beneficial to the employer or the partner than the woman.

"I will leave a job," she says. "I will also leave a relationship."

This is a sign, perhaps, of generational change, a result of young women observing the way certain struggles unfolded for the older generation and wanting no part of it.

Often, our personal observations influence the choices we make. You learn from a grandmother who bought elegant dresses but had no place to wear them because her husband kept her isolated. Or an aunt who never remarried after her husband died but joined every dance group and tai chi class she could find, staying energized well into her 90s. We make decisions based on role models, whether they are celebrities divorcing unappreciative husbands or our mothers.

"For months, [my mother] had been talking about wanting to retire," Stephanie says. "She was underpaid, and her experience was terrible, but she said, 'I don't have a pension and I'm terrified to make the leap.' And something in me said, 'Stephanie, don't you ever find yourself in your 50s or 60s afraid to throw in the towel.' I thought, 'I never want to be in a situation where I can't live comfortably after working.' The fear that I saw in her face pained me, because there was nothing that I could do for her, trying to raise my daughter and take care of my own household.

"I thought that is no way to live. I totally get wanting to hold on to [a job] that is good, but if there is something else out there that is better, then I am willing to put whatever I need to put on the line in pursuit of that."

In her Lainey Gossip column, Stephanie uses storylines of the rich and famous to highlight universal issues. After Emily Ratajkowski, the American model, actress, mother, and author, filed for divorce from her apparently wayward husband in 2023, she told fans that no matter how beautiful a woman may be, some men will always cheat. That created, or expanded, a public conversation about the value of an early exit.

As Stephanie wrote in her October 2023 column, "According to EmRata, the benefits of divorcing before you hit 30 . . . include having your own money and still having your whole life, and so much energy, ahead of you."

This attitude is heralded by some young women, and the same wish for independence is found among many who are decades older. When Stephanie opened her column with a discussion on the growing desire to live alone, in peace, she cited 1990s Canadian supermodel Linda Evangelista who, when asked by *The Sunday Times* if she wanted to date again, said, "Not interested. I don't want to sleep with anybody anymore. I don't want to hear somebody breathing." Stephanie also noted Whoopi Goldberg's comments in a 2016 *New York Times Magazine* interview: After three marriages, she said she was not particularly interested in the institution or in dating. "I'm much happier on my own," Goldberg said. "I can spend as much time with somebody as I want to spend, but I'm not looking to be with somebody forever or live with someone. I don't want somebody in my house."

"Whoopi and Linda are saying the *same* damn thing," Stephanie's column said. "Not wanting to hear anyone breathe or snore, not wanting anyone in your house, it all drives home the point that these women, and *so* many others, truly enjoy their solitude."

However anecdotal, there is truth to this statement. A wife-seeking man in his early 60s said most of the women he meets are divorced and so happy to be free that he's having a hard time finding any takers. The pursuit of solitude seems real, but in statistical terms it is an undeniable fact that as women grow older — and their men die — they will live solo. Chosen or not, aloneness is part of older women's experiences. Among Canadian women aged 75 and older, 41.5 percent lived alone in 2021, compared to 20 percent of men.

There is, of course, a caveat to highlighting the chosen singledom of supermodels and celebrities. As Stephanie pointed out in her column, "We don't all have the luxury of being able to afford the independence these women say they're after."

It is a lot easier to embrace freedom when you have the income for a fabulous house and a grand social life, not to mention vacations in the south of France or wherever it is that celebrities take their respite.

For many women, especially those whose years in the workforce have ended, independence comes with a devastating cost. Susan Patricia Staples, the 76-year-old from Ottawa who on occasion sleeps in her car, says her most painful "mentoring" conversations are those with women who want to leave abusive partners and realize that with freedom comes something akin to poverty. "They have a tough choice," she says.

The long-term impact of relationship toxicity is immeasurable, and yet so many hold on, steeling themselves against the stress that can downgrade the body on a cellular level and potentially raise the risk of cancer or further its spread.

Chronic stress can come from many sources: a bad boss, diminished health, financial downfall, or a partner who is a pathological liar. For women without the means, the outcome of leaving a spouse and selling a house or letting go of an apartment can lead to an unaffordable existence, so many choose to stay.

This is why Stephanie plans to protect her money. If she is disposable to an employer, she believes in a relationship, the risk is greater. "If I walked away from this company, they'd have a new me tomorrow. If I walk away from a man, he'll find someone new and younger by next week," she says.

It's all relative, the way society and some men view women. Pat Dunn, the woman in her 70s who wears thrift-store blouses with elegance, gave up dating after an older man told her he prefers women from a lower age bracket. Stephanie, 40 years younger than Pat, has reached the same conclusion on her value as a woman in her mid-30s and about the labour performed by women for their man.

"You're hearing all of these anecdotes about women being in just godawful marriages," she says. "I think it is the implications of heterosexual marriages specifically and the glaring gap between men's ability to really understand the work that women do in and outside of the household and their ability to properly acknowledge that. I hear that from a lot of married women, and it doesn't sell me on the idea of marriage," she says. "I can finance a life on my own — one that I prefer."

When a former romantic partner told Stephanie that independence will leave her "alone and rotting with your cat," she looked at him and said, "I can't think of a better way to spend my fucking life."

"Every night after I put my daughter to bed," she says, "I make a cup of tea, or I pour a glass of wine and I snuggle up with my cat, watching my shows. I don't have to worry about some man coming in here and talking to me about the hard day he had.

"I've really started to value my independence, and it might cost a lot more than if I was sharing a home or a life with somebody. But every day it proves to be more and more worth it. And we're seeing all these famous women who are leaving their husbands and going on to flourish."

These are the insights that called Stephanie into the Lainey Gossip galaxy. Lainey Lui, the Canadian entrepreneur, *etalk* anchor, former host on *The Social*, and purveyor of in-depth celebrity analysis, hired Stephanie for her take on women's finances, dating apps, and the Real Housewives. Her discussions may begin with a recap of last week's *Housewives* episode, but they also connect with racial issues, careers, finances, and single motherhood.

And Stephanie's refusal to be shamed for having so-called failed relationships connects with readers, Lainey says, many of whom do not see themselves reflected in a world that demands a perfect trajectory through life, with a forever marriage.

By sharing her life, Stephanie defies the damning beliefs, however unspoken, that tell women to stay quiet and stick with a partner no matter how toxic or be judged as inadequate. It is a perfectly manicured middle finger to the societal smugness that suggests longevity in a relationship matters more than peace of mind.

Stephanie believes that her approach to serious topics engages women who do not see themselves elevated on large platforms, be they racialized or be they those who had to fight longer than others to find their place in the workforce.

Some get jobs through family connections, she notes, and never understand the grit it takes for others to arrive, usually years later. Stephanie got her "real" job at the age of 31. The delay in a good salary and pension is the reason why, at least for now, she has no plans for a second child.

"Just the hit that you take to your career to bring life into the world is a lot. It's immeasurable," she says. "And it feels thankless almost, because even when I was at home on mat leave, I was still also responsible to cook and to clean, and you know, the work that you do is so invisible.

"My plan is very much to charge ahead on the career front and go as far as I possibly can and show my daughter that she can do the same.

"Her poor boyfriends have no idea what they're up against because the vetting process for them will be 'Are you a narcissist? Are you a manipulator? Are you going to make my daughter feel like she has to have sex with you?' I was there. I need her to see that she does not need any of that shit. She can do whatever she wants to do. I'll finance the entire thing. Just be true to you."

After Stephanie raises the topic of men with narcissistic tendencies, the soft-spoken manipulators, the sweet liars, we discuss the prevalence of those who fit the cluster B personality disorders in the American Psychiatric Association's *Diagnostic and Statistical Manual of Mental Disorders, Fifth Edition*. "Oh, they are everywhere," she says.

Our discussion shifts to a Facebook group Stephanie joined called Are We Dating the Same Guy?, otherwise known as AWDTSG, an acronym that honestly isn't worth the struggle. In what would have been a great Carrie Bradshaw column, the AWDTSG group originated in Manhattan in 2022 and has since spread across the United States and Canada, with millions of members in local groups from Newfoundland to all major cities westward.

These are private sites that require permission to join from the administrators and a question on, for example, the number one rule for admission; if not answered perfectly, the request to join is denied.

For Stephanie, AWDTSG has become a support group born from feminine intuition, the natural inclination to investigate when instinct says men are behaving badly. Not all men, of course.

Many are lovely humans, but apparently there are enough missing the integrity gene that tens of thousands of women in the Toronto region alone perfected the answer to that skill-testing question and joined.

Not all the reviews for the AWDTSG group are great, with some Reddit chats saying its comments are increasingly catty, but for Stephanie, it's an online forum that outs some questionable characters (using dating app photographs) and brings the solace of sisterhood.

"People have found their husbands in there. Someone said, 'Is anyone dating this man?' And another woman said, 'Yeah, we've been married for 17 years.' Imagine that."

She likens its value to employer checks when job seeking. There are a lot of online review sites that rate corporate treatment of staff; with a guy, she says, especially someone from the anonymous world of dating apps, who vouches for that person?

"What I love is that it's not usually the women fighting each other, if it's like, 'Oh, we're both dating the same guy.' [It's] 'Well, he's a piece of shit, and I'm going to make sure that I cut things off with him.' I think it's a fantastic resource for women to be able to just do a community check to make sure that they are safe, because going on a date with a man for the first time can be very, very dangerous. And this really helps to mitigate that. So, I just spend time in that group and I'm like, oh my God, look at this community. It's great, although the men are very upset about it.

"And now there are so many comments from women saying, 'I just don't think that dating is right for me. I used to want to get married, but there's just so much shit out there. I think I want to ride this out alone.' I'm seeing that narrative increase time and time again and I'm like, Welcome to the club."

All of which brings us back to Whoopi and Linda.

These are two older women who have declared they are done. That may change, of course. We have all made such definitive statements and sometimes, quite wonderfully, someone worthy comes along. But at least for now, they've committed to aloneness, like so many others.

It is worth recognizing women who struggle with the choice of independence over survival. Staying in a relationship offers a place to live. A stove. A warm shower. And shared expenses. It is much harder to leave an abusive or manipulative relationship when the outside options are so few and so expensive, even for those with equity in a house. Some women never leave.

As Stephanie wrote on Lainey Gossip, "So though a *lot* of us may be silently (or loudly) agreeing with Linda and Whoopi, we know that going it alone is a tough choice, and certainly an expensive one, particularly as we age."

It can be soul-crushing, she says, to recognize that so many women remain in relationships because housing is too expensive to manage alone.

"As a single parent, it's a cost I know very well. And though I don't have the wealth of Linda or Whoopi, I'm lucky enough to get by because solitude gives me a lot of agency, and to me, it's worth every penny."

Start saving, sisters. There's no one more powerful than a woman of independent means.

CHAPTER SEVEN

Susan

It was decades ago, when she was in her 40s, that Susan Patricia Staples discovered the comfort of sleeping in her car, not due to financial deprivation, not yet. Back in the 1990s, it was her desire to make space for the women who shared her lover's home.

Funny how unconventional relationships transform life, Susan likes to say, laughing at the irony that she, an early wave feminist who spent years with a lesbian partner became devoted to a truly androcentric existence, a world that upheld a man.

Susan fell in love with his mind. So did the others who already lived with him when she arrived, and while also men were part of the community, he was the leader. Together, they created an artistic enclave of sorts in a Pennsylvanian forest and later travelled through Europe performing classical theatre. Susan does not want his name used, saying he had been approached to star in a documentary about his life, his art, his women and children but pointedly and definitively declined.

Let's call him R. According to his obituary, R. was an accomplished man, educated at Howard University, and well-known in the international arts community. With his women, he raised a lot of children. Susan had one son from an ex-husband, and while she counted Ottawa as her permanent home, her extended visits to this little community tucked in the woods meant that in many ways her boy grew up in R.'s world. It was a place where children were considered art rats, not rug rats. They played without adult-imposed structure and were part of dinner discussions on the lives of Trojans or the triple goddesses of Greek tragedy. It was here that boys and girls learned about the life passage of women from the maiden, represented by a full moon, to the mother, the crescent moon, to the crone, considered a waning moon. (Many women now contest the waning descriptor, preferring a fresh version of the rising moon.)

R. is eight years gone now. Susan still grieves. She feels lost without him.

She once told him that she wanted to invite an anthropologist to live in their little community and study their large clan and kinship group. It crossed class, gender, race, and age. In Susan's opinion, the women who loved R. shared him without jealousy. It was that unusual, she'd say. R. told her to go ahead with her anthropological curiosity but, in no rush, he died before she got started, a regret that stings to this day.

It is his other women whose friendships now sustain her. In some ways that may sound remarkable; to Susan, it is not surprising. The community was defined by R. and it revolved around him, but it could not have thrived without the women's energy.

She is in her mid-70s now, and from her tiny subsidized Ottawa apartment, Susan is drawn there still, yearning for the final stretch of road that winds toward the big house, its doors open wide.

The year after he died, Susan drove south, sleeping for free in parks or on side roads, her internal compass set to the home she shared with R.'s partners, where her grief and theirs mixed in the embrace of the feminine. It was the women, once again, who outlasted their man.

In the spring of 2024, after a knee replacement in the winter, Susan was worried. Could she manage that drive? The pain had knocked her out for months. It's hard to crawl into the back of a Grand Caravan for a night's sleep when you can't move without a walker.

Her old red Ford Focus, the car she lived in during those nine months of poverty in 2018, is gone now, replaced by the used van. Susan's son was working in California during her first run at car life. He helped her buy the van after a bit of a freakout when he learned, many months after the fact, that his mom had been sleeping in her vehicle.

At the time, in her late 60s, Susan had been just managing, running a little after-school tutoring club in a community centre that provided a marginal income, enough to pay rent and buy groceries. As it happens, one family unexpectedly moved out of the city, after the new school year began, pulling their three children from the program. It's just one of those things, no one is at fault, she says, but the loss of that income felt like a gut punch. Her son would have sent money, but Susan didn't tell him. Let your children be free, she believes.

At home, in her apartment, she looked around at the simple furnishings and decided it was a pretty enough package to sublet, furnished, at least for a year. After all, she had slept in her car before, admittedly under much different circumstances. Susan decided to go all the way and this time live in it. What could go wrong? With her son so far away, there was no need to tell anyone she had created her own version of affordable housing.

Car life, as she calls it, was an unintentional outcome of her years with R., and thank the goddesses, because it has given her the freedom to survive in hard times and travel when she has a very basic home but little extra money, as she does now. There is nothing worse, she says, than being stuck inside four walls, unable to be part of the world.

Susan's Ottawa apartment is part of non-profit housing created by a local church, with apartments and, for those with higher needs, built-in supports. She moved in at the higher rent of $1,200 a month, which was barely affordable, but later managed to get a subsidy, saving about $350 per month. She lives on $1,988 from a minimal CPP payment, the Guaranteed Income Supplement, and Old Age Security, which is higher than average because, in a well-executed plan of self-restraint, she held off taking it until the age of 70. "It makes a difference," she tells women. Susan does not love living here, but she is grateful, especially to the friend who put her name on the wait-list nearly 20 years ago.

The inspiration for Susan's vehicular version of freedom began back in the early days of her relationship with R. She wanted her own space in the home she came to visit, so she created a bed in the back of her car. He teased her for leaving him at night, but to Susan, sleeping outdoors with the windows cracked open and the fireflies sparkling in the trees gave her an independence that has never withered. Until now.

Susan is hoping to make that drive again. It keeps getting delayed, but the plan is to visit friends in Nova Scotia and wind south toward Maine where she will park overnight along the beaches until turning inland, toward her ultimate destination.

Living in a car is not easy, and complications grow with age. Her knee replacement is still healing, and in the early months after surgery, she could barely speak, the pain mixed with fear was too much. She ended up with dangerously low blood pressure that required hospitalization; which led to a more sedentary life than she anticipated and added stress on her back, where osteoarthritis has long been her greatest source of pain. It was a downward cascade of problems, one creating the next, leaving Susan in a state of fragility. She does not like it one bit. Even worse is the neuropathy in her feet and legs, a new addition to Susan's health woes, related to her diabetes. Neuropathy, with its tingling and numbness, could lead to a wheelchair.

This is not the life she had planned, and to be sure, no one ever really knows how the years will surprise the body. How do you anticipate the possibilities that might unfold? Susan, with characteristic bluntness, is aware that her weight, at 212 pounds, is another problem. "I am fat," she says lightly.

Some people have had good luck moving through the years like Susan, an original hippie, who never felt the need to renounce her beliefs for wealth. She got a university degree in social work but left the profession, she says, to avoid becoming an instrument of the system that inevitably institutionalizes the people it seeks to help. Now that her son is married and living in Ottawa with his wife, Susan had hoped to help them by investing her time in their lives, saving them $30 a day on dog-walking fees, since she has no money to help with anything else. It is hard enough to take care of the dog while using a walker, but what happens if she ends up in a wheelchair? And how could she help if they have a baby? Susan asks this question and sits in silence. This new life phase is not what she envisioned.

Not everyone would agree with her position, certainly not advocates for the vulnerable, but Susan says she would happily embrace medical assistance in dying before leading a life of full dependency, reliant on someone else for washing, eating, and moving from bed to chair. Some call that ableism. For Susan, it is pragmatic.

Her travels were supposed to begin in June. She got her clothes organized, her travel kit packed, and she planned to start driving as far as her knee and neuropathy would take her. She hoped on the first day to make it to Drummondville, Quebec, which at roughly three hours from Ottawa is not that far, but Susan is in no rush. She might stop at an overnight camping spot, though these days she finds decent campgrounds have padded their prices, sometimes to as much as $70 a night, which was once the cost of a basic hotel room. So, if the accommodations do not fit her budget, Susan boondocks, pulling her van into a park, sleeping on her upholstery foam bed. It is more dangerous now than her original nights outdoors, with her lover's visits. In many cities, particularly in the U.S., new anti-homeless laws make car life increasingly difficult, as does the vulnerability of sleeping in a vehicle, to say nothing of the heat that can cause strokes, especially in older bodies.

Though this existence offers a way to survive, it is not necessarily a romantic life of freedom. Yes, the car has a roof that protects Susan from the elements, but it does not wrap a woman in safety from strangers, not the way a sturdy building might, depending, of course, on who is inside it. When Susan lived in her Ford Focus for that nine-month stretch, she mostly slept in well-lit parking lots or on side streets in good neighbourhoods; it got tricky on hot nights when the windows needed to stay open to allow a breeze inside. For protection, she attached a little vial of pepper spray and a wailing safety alarm to a bungee cord near her head so if anyone leaned inside her car, she could quietly reach up with her right hand and gather her weapons, however benign. Once, a man rifled through the contents of the passenger seat, and she awakened with a blast, screaming. He banged his head, exiting, and stood outside, panting. Susan lay inside, panting. She peered out the window as he stood there, terribly thin, his body twitching, jerky. Susan screamed, "Go away!" He did. After that night, it was clear that the Velcro and netting protected against bugs but not humans. She started parking in McDonald's and Walmart lots alongside big recreational vehicles or other women in cars, close enough to feel secure without invading anyone's space.

This was Susan's learning period. She bought a $24 membership to an Ottawa community centre on a seniors' discount. It gave her access to the washrooms for a morning shower, which was also a good way to clean her long flowy dresses. It offered air conditioning or heat, depending on the season. During this period of homelessness, when she had sublet the apartment she could no longer afford but didn't want to lose, Susan was fortunate enough to identify the holy grail of washrooms. It was a single room with a reliably locked door that offered a personal hygiene system: disinfect the sink and toilet with Lysol wipes, the kind that would later run out during the pandemic, and strip down for a full sponge bath and a shampoo.

This kind of morning ritual may be more common than most realize, since older women are still invisible at least to those who are oblivious to what they are seeing. From Susan's perspective, if there's a woman in the washroom early in the morning brushing her teeth or washing her face, she's probably living in her car.

These days, she has a portable toilet that sits in the back of her van, beside her bed in case she needs to use it in the middle of the night. "I'm pretty hooked up," she says happily. It is called the Dometic, a sturdy creation that gets 4.5 stars on Amazon, and it flushes, holding the contents in a five-gallon basin.

She adds two TST citrus tabs, sold at Canadian Tire, to eliminate odours in recreational vehicle toilets, and as such, there is no smell. Of course, the Dometic has to be emptied, so she sometimes stops at one of those unaffordable campgrounds because they allow dumping on the cheap, usually $10, at least in the U.S. While there, she fills jugs with non-potable water, which is good for bathing.

It requires significant advance planning, but in her opinion, car life is immeasurably better than living in a homeless shelter. Always hold on to your vehicle, no matter how old, and keep it in a good state of repair — that's Susan's mantra to struggling women.

Still, it is hard to say how many are ready for this existence. While finding a parking spot is increasingly difficult, one of the greatest challenges to car life is first getting your mind around the idea of living inside a vehicle, sleeping so exposed. It is public, isolating, and potentially dangerous. For many women, the shift seems near impossible, although looking at Facebook, it appears to be a growing phenomenon, however hidden from the mainstream.

When she talks to women online, Susan tries to offer little tips that help people envision nomadic success. She can take a two-gallon jug of water and, in a long dress, crouch in the bushes and wash herself in all the right places without ever being exposed. There are parks where there is hardly anybody around, she tells them. "That's where you go off on your own," she tells them. "You wash your genitals and your armpits and stuff under the dress." She can also sit in her car, remove her bra, and change into pajamas without any exposure.

On Facebook, Susan sees more older women making a life on the road and sharing tips. In the winter, when it is too cold to wash outdoors, some find a big truck stop and pay for a private shower. There is always a solution. Each day is focused on survival.

There are many reasons why women are in this lifestyle, and from reading the Facebook comments, it is often unemployment or the lack of money to pay for the rising cost of rent. Sometimes, it is the brutal combination of low income and intimate partner violence, whether emotional or physical. That decision, to stay in a toxic home or live in a car, is not always one that friends understand. It is a hard choice to either stay with abuse that tears into your body or leave it behind for this unlikely world of nomads.

Susan believes the life of auto-nomadics, as her son calls them, is not as strange as it appears, because there is a community of people who support each other online and sometimes in person, finding places to meet, however fleetingly. We all need companionship, and auto-nomadics are no different. Isolation is built into that life, but you can also be lonely in a nice house with a man whose soul is raging.

Just because you live on the road, Susan says, doesn't mean you lose the desire for love or sex; you just need to find the right tribe.

Susan found hers in that big house in the forest. She needs the strength now to get back there.

HOUSING FACTS

In 2024, more than 80,000 Ontarians experienced homelessness, whether staying in emergency shelters or outdoor spaces, according to the Association of Municipalities of Ontario. This number does not account for the hidden homeless, such as those living in cars.

Earlier data, from the 2021 Canadian Housing Survey published by Statistics Canada, found that 10 percent of respondents (of all ages and genders) said they have lived temporarily with family, friends, in a car, or another location. More than half were women. Among all respondents, 14 percent were aged 65 and older.

The U.S. National Homelessness Law Center says car life is dangerous and prone to encounters with police and vigilantes, a particular problem for those who are racialized or members of the 2SLGBTQI+ community.

CHAPTER EIGHT

The Cars

Dr. Amanda Grenier has spent her career focused on people who exist in financial precarity or those who no longer have a place to live. It's a harrowing world, even with years of perspective. Dr. Grenier is a professor at the University of Toronto's Factor-Inwentash Faculty of Social Work and researcher at the Baycrest Academy for Research and Education. The author of *Late-Life Homelessness: Experiences of Disadvantage and Unequal Aging*, she embarked in 2024 upon a five-year research project to examine a measurement for poverty that best reflects the needs of older adults. Much of her work is focused on older women.

So, I sought Dr. Grenier's perspective on the experience of Canadian women living in vehicles, who are unlikely to be chronically homeless, as evidenced by the fact that they have a car. As Susan Patricia Staples says, it's big step above sleeping on the sidewalk.

There are downward steps that we take toward a life exposed to the streets, whether in a shelter or a vehicle. It could start with couch surfing and shift to a rooming house before the shelter or sidewalk. It's endless, exhausting transition.

"The car that keeps moving is a piece of that because you don't know where you belong, you're excluded from the population. And you keep moving," Dr. Grenier says. "We can speculate on why people might choose to live in a car. One is because they have the car. It's already been purchased. They can't afford housing. They've been displaced for whatever reason, which might be an eviction, a divorce, or intimate partner violence. So, the car becomes that only option."

It's the only source of stability, this home on wheels. The bigger question here, which few consider because no one really talks about this growing phenomenon, is the displacement of older women. Wives and mothers. Our nurturers, co-workers, mentors.

From a sociological perspective, I ask Dr. Grenier what the move into a car says about this world of ours, about us.

"I think that's the question," she says. "What does it say about society that people are making these difficult choices between environments that are not designed for aging? Whether that's an emergency room, a shelter, the street, or a car, they're not places that are designed for good, healthy aging and well-being later in life. And so, is this the society that we want? Is that just? I would say it violates any principle of human rights and justice."

• • •

In the beginning, humans were wanderers.

They travelled with a tribe, a group who protected each other from the dangers of the times. Those who ventured off alone, or were sent away, didn't always fare well.

According to the Online Etymology Dictionary, the word *nomad* originated in the 1550s to describe "a wanderer, one of a tribe of people who have no fixed abode." While hunter-gatherers still exist, humans have, over the millennia, grown to favour permanency. First, in agricultural communities; later, in cities. In Canada, settlers came from away, usually with plans to build a home; in periods of great recession, sometimes combined with drought, many had to move.

We often associate the stock market crash of 1929 and the ensuing dust bowl with photographs shot by Dorothea Lange, the American photojournalist known for images of people living in cars or tents, struggling to survive. Her most famous photograph is called *Migrant Mother*, depicting a woman named Florence Thompson, living in a tent with her children. The dust bowl hit the Canadian prairies, too, and workers who came from afar, hoping to settle on a farm or in a rural town, had to leave to look for new jobs across the country.

Many recessions have followed, some consequential, others less so. Perhaps the worst in recent times happened in 2008, when the U.S. housing bubble led to a stock market crash that took down a lot of Americans. They lost retirement savings and homes in what became known as the predatory subprime mortgage crisis. With little left, many held on to their vehicles, the most beloved of American possessions, and drove across the country looking for work, which is the story that journalist Jessica Bruder told in her book *Nomadland*.

With stricter government oversight of lending practices, Canadians escaped that particular economic disaster, rather smugly. But the ensuing escalation of housing costs, whether buying or renting, soon spiralled into a crisis. In many ways, this deep period of unaffordability is a pain shared across the border.

Among older people, particularly women who face a significant gender pension gap, the near impossible expense of renting has created a new cohort of impoverished.

In Canada, a nation that prefers discretion, we don't much talk about women in survival mode. In the U.S., the discussion of car life long ago shifted from shock to a debate over word choices and why they matter. Vehicular *homelessness* is also known as vehicular *residency*, depending on one's perspective on whether car life is forced or chosen.

A growing number of people are sufficiently adrift that the embrace of this no-fixed-address existence provides them a certain stability, says anthropologist and California housing strategist Dr. Graham Pruss. In a 2023 paper, Pruss argued that vehicle residency should be officially considered a viable form of long-term housing, though most government policies do not.

In Washington, D.C., at the National Homelessness Law Center, policy director and lawyer Eric Tars calls car life vehicular homelessness. It may be a choice for those seeking a life on the road, but for many, says Tars, it is an unwanted solution to indigence in their later years.

"These are people who have worked their entire lives but are now living on a fixed income, whether it's a pension or Social Security or disability income, but that income isn't enough to keep up with the skyrocketing cost of rent and other expenses," say Tars. "In the U.S., we don't have universal health care. So, in Florida, for example, one survey found that unpaid medical debt was the number one cause of homelessness. And seniors who have these rising medical costs that they can't keep up with end up becoming homeless."

Canada's universal medicine is not perfect. In many regions, there are shortages of family physicians. Some patients wait hours in hospital emergency departments for treatment. Ultimately, most get the care they need. It is deeply alarming to hear of Americans going bankrupt from health care expenses, and it is also a cautionary tale, as some Canadian provinces try to shift medical procedures to private clinics, which might include added costs.

In many American communities, the rising cost of housing and health care has created a noxious mix for some older people, making it near impossible to survive. As Tars says, the vehicle is the last option. And yet many communities don't want people sleeping in cars. Local governments are passing bylaws that make it difficult to park overnight. That sends some people to the outskirts of town alone, where risks abound. A National Homelessness Law Center survey of 187 cities found that 43 percent prohibit sleeping in vehicles, a 119 percent increase between 2011 and 2019.

And yet for many, as Pruss's paper argues, living in a car has become a legitimate way of life, particularly when there are few alternatives. Americans, he wrote, are using their private property — vehicles — to create affordable housing.

Instead of aspiring to a retirement in a nice brick bungalow filled with possessions, vehicle residents focus on minimalism and budgetary bliss, and it helps to be handy with an engine. Humans being human, car life also comes with status symbols. It could be a really cool retro trailer cap on a Ram pickup. Or a portable toilet system that is superior to a more basic version that uses ziplocked baggies. There is also a hierarchy, a celebrity culture. At the peak is Bob Wells, with long white hair and a beard, who has a YouTube channel with some 800,000 followers, watching as he describes the freedom of an "apartment on wheels."

Wells founded an annual festival called Rubber Tramp Rendezvous in Quartzsite, Arizona, a massive winter community of vehicle dwellers that *Nomadland* explored to much acclaim. In his research, Pruss has spent hours interviewing people at Quartzsite and smaller communities across California. While I imagined them yearning for the comforts of a house or apartment, Pruss says many speak with disdain for traditional housing, what they contemptuously call "bricks and sticks."

This is how people adapt to the times in which they live. With a growing number of Americans aging out of jobs and relying on limited Social Security payments, their options decrease. Survival becomes increasingly tenuous with the cuts to Social Security, Medicare, and Medicaid, health care for low-income Americans.

In the U.S., where successes and failures always seem greater, there is much research on car life, particularly in California, including Pruss's paper "Homes Without Homes." It cites research that estimates one million Americans live in vehicles, parking on streets, in public lots, and at parks. In 2019, in Los Angeles County, an estimated 16,528 people, or 37 percent of those reported as unsheltered, lived in a vehicle, he noted. In Seattle and King County in Washington State, the number of people living in vehicles grew from 852 (30 percent of the unsheltered population) in 2009 to 3,372 (53 percent of the unsheltered population) in 2018. Whether people are living in their cars by choice or desperation, those numbers are on the rise.

Pruss has dedicated his academic and professional career to housing issues in part because of his own experience of homelessness as a youth and use of social services as a teenaged father. That background led to years of volunteering and professional experience "with people who live in public spaces, particularly in vehicles," his paper says.

Even with his personal experience, it took Pruss time to appreciate the difference in philosophies between housing advocates, like himself, and those in the vehicle-dwelling world. As already noted, the terms *vehicular homelessness* and *vehicular residency* have disparate meanings, and both are used by advocates fighting to improve living conditions.

So, I asked Pruss, What gives?

Vehicular homelessness, he says, is a term he coined many years ago, while working as an outreach worker in Seattle with a caseload of about 1,500 people living in cars or vans.

"The people who I worked with, by and large, matched the category of homelessness," Pruss says. "That's what we would generally call them. But over and over they were telling me, 'I'm not homeless. That [the vehicle] is my home.'

"And, you know, it took almost a decade for me to actually accept that, I'm not proud to say. I was working in the system and I was like, 'Yeah, but you're really homeless and we've got to get you out of this vehicle.'"

As he did his post-doctoral research and travelled across California, speaking with people living in vehicles, including those with enough money to live and travel in recreational vehicles, Pruss repeatedly heard the same words: "I'm. Not. Homeless."

"And then going out to Arizona and hearing these stories again but from people who are even more affluent," says Pruss, "that led to this realization that there needed to be a better term than *vehicular homeless*, because many who are in this, not only do they not self-identify as homeless, but it denies their home. It is their legal property, and it is their home. And that is why I started adopting the term *vehicle residency*, and *vehicle resident*."

He believes this large group, with many subcultures from the wealthier to the adventurers and the impoverished, holds an economic power that should be recognized, particularly for the seasonal labour provided in farming, campgrounds, and warehousing. The list of employers that rely on so-called itinerant labour is so long that the community holds job recruiting sessions in Quartzsite. And yet, Pruss says, the federal government still considers vehicle dwellers to be homeless.

There is a non-political push from the National Vehicle Residency Collective, the non-profit organization he works with, for dwellers to vote in federal elections; without a permanent address, municipal voting is not an option.

Unaffordability has forced many out of "bricks and sticks" housing, but over time, some grow accustomed to a life without debt. Bob Wells speaks on social media about freedom, saying the rest of us have bought into a big lie that keeps us enslaved to mortgages or high rent. Given the price of housing, at least in large cities, it is hard to argue against the theory that many of us are indentured servants to big banks.

It is also not so easy to romanticize a life in which great thought must be given to every bodily function, every day, let alone to finding a safe place to sleep where one is not tormented by unwelcoming neighbours or a random dude trying to break into the car. The summer heat can make you sick, and the winter cold can be unbearable without an Arctic Shield sleeping bag. For some, every day is a fight.

As an anthropologist, Pruss uses the big tent theory, which allows for a widely inclusive cast of characters, when asked if car life is painted more glowingly than reality suggests. Some who live in RVs are more affluent, he says, living nicely on retirement pensions or earning a good salary while working remotely. Others would much rather live in an affordable apartment but cannot pay rent *and* buy groceries. It's one or the other. So, they adapt, stepping outside the traditional walls and travelling the country, paying a lot less for gas than rent.

"Often, the story is deeply entrenched in the housing market," Pruss says. "It is very much a story of displacement, unaffordability, and, in a larger sense, of discontent, people who do not want to put their money toward paying off a landlord's mortgage, or they may not like the community they are living in and want to find something different."

In the U.S. and Canada, the overarching issues are the same, with housing costs being the main issue; the challenges for women might be more intense in the U.S. given the greater gender pension gap. In 2022, Canada's gender pension gap, which is defined as the difference between the retirement income of men and women, was 22 percent, according to the OECD, while in the U.S., it was nearly 34 percent. In Canada, the combination of Old Age Security and Guaranteed Income Supplement, for those on a very low income, gives a small monthly boost. This is not meant to serve as a cross-border analysis of retirement living since the differences are complex.

Many older women Pruss meets in his research are displaced and the reasons are, at least in part, related to gender. "There are a growing number of older women in the U.S. who are aging into Social Security or some other form of retirement, and because of a historic gender wage gap, because of a divorce, and having a retirement fund taken away from them or because they were not an earner who paid into Social Security, they may not be getting all of the benefits from it," he says.

By the time they reach their late 60s, the choices are limited, especially for those relying on Social Security payments, which are based on how much each individual paid into the system during their working years, somewhat similar to Canada's CPP. Of course, women in America also stayed at home with children or worked lower-paying jobs so their retirement income is often limited.

"It is virtually impossible to live anywhere in the U.S. for $700 a month," he says, citing an oft-used figure for an average monthly Social Security payment. "It's extremely difficult. And they are seeing that if they have to live on $700 a month, it's going to mean that they really can't do anything else. They're sort of afraid to go outside, because what if you break a leg? Or how can you afford to buy a coffee? You can't go to a movie if you can't even afford to eat.

"And so they're sort of stuck inside the 'sticks and bricks.' There's a very strong perspective that the housing market is broken and people are using their vehicles as an alternative that better suits their needs. I'm not trying to make that claim myself, but I hear so many people responding to these problems for those reasons."

Quartzsite's Rubber Tramp Rendezvous has a separate gathering just for women. The 2023 calendar of events had sessions for women's hygiene, interior decorating for "homes on wheels," and "maintaining healthy boundaries." At the main event, there were talks on chronic illness, estate planning, a screening of *Nomadland*, and an opportunity to meet Bob Wells.

Vehicular residency has been quantified in many American cities, particularly on the West Coast, but in Canada, it still seems to be a more solitary pursuit. Without warm winters and famous destination sites, the cars and the women inside slip unnoticed into the night.

CHAPTER NINE

Pat

In 2003, Pat and Dave paid $200,000 for a boat, a 55-foot-long diesel-operated trawler called *H&E Hope*. Pat used her leftover proceeds from the house sale and cashed in RRSPs and other savings to cover her share. It was an older trawler with a walkway on the outer rim and more room than a sailboat, perfect for two people who wanted enough space to keep the love alive. Made of steel, *H&E Hope* was built by a boat maker for his family, and when it didn't feel big enough, he lopped off the stern and added another 10 feet, a bit of maritime lore that Pat and Dave loved.

They docked at Port Credit in Mississauga and later, when Dave started working in Kitchener, moved to Hamilton Harbour. Those were good times. Nothing like an evening under the stars with fellow boaters, a friendly group known for their love of good wine, especially when the water was calm. Dave had a dream. At least Pat thought it belonged to him. It might have been hers too. In their mid-60s, they would retire and take *H&E Hope* down the eastern seaboard of America and into the Caribbean, with a short sojourn on Grand Cayman Island, where Pat's daughter lived, and head into the Panama Canal and out the other side to the Galapagos Islands. "I want to see the dinosaurs," Pat would say of the islands' ancient wildlife, and Dave would smile indulgently.

In 2004, after 14 years with a decent salary and government benefits, Pat left her job as a public health nurse. She had been unhappy for a time and spoke to Dave about her desire for change. He knew a thing or two about switching corporate jobs and landing on his feet, leaving IBM for other opportunities; his work often focused on quality control and safety standards. He suggested Pat go into consulting for health and safety so she started a little company and made good money until 2008 when, during the recession, businesses started cutting back. With her consulting company failing, and a $90,000 inheritance from her mother in her bank account, Pat looked for a new opportunity.

Dave suggested a tanning salon as a smart long-term investment, but Pat the nurse told him she could not in good conscience make money by putting people at risk of skin cancer. Instead, she decided to buy a café in Hamilton, one that had been a long-time fixture in a downtown office building. Again, it's all about timing. Many of the businesses in that building lost money, and one after another started leaving. Coffee-addicted office staff were in short supply. At the same time, Pat realized she had been too trusting. She hadn't hired an accountant to check the financials of the coffee shop before buying it. "Worst mistake of my life." Instead of selling the café, which would have required fudging the numbers to find a buyer, an act she refused to commit, Pat sold off the kitchen equipment at a loss.

She wanted a change. Dave wanted to retire. They had already invested thousands of dollars on new electronics for *H&E Hope*, creating what Pat called a "tickety-boo" navigation system for safety on the open seas. So, in the fall of 2011, as the hurricane season ended, Pat and Dave's great Caribbean adventure began.

At first, they hung close to the East Coast, sailing up the Hudson River to New York City. Pat got a crick in her neck from staring in awe at the skyline. They dropped anchor near the Statue of Liberty. Later, long past Key West, that electronic navigational system alerted them to an incoming hurricane. It forced a stop in Cuba and eight hours of questioning from an assortment of government officials checking off questions on official documents, including a veterinarian who filled out his governmental forms without once looking at their goldendoodle, Dood. Eventually a man who trimmed his beard Castro-style gave them the go-ahead to shelter in Cuban territory. Like the other boaters, they headed to a mangrove where local sailors were diving for lobsters. Surfacing with handfuls of crustaceans, they told the Canadians to fire up the barbie.

The storm veered west so the next morning, Pat and Dave waved goodbye to their Cuban friends and began the trip to Grand Cayman, the largest of the three Cayman Islands, a long, gut-chucking trip at five miles an hour with a diesel engine on the open ocean. It was around this time that Pat noticed Dave's hands as he gripped the helm. They were swollen and red, and the skin stretched tight across his knuckles. As the waves roiled the boat, Dave stopped eating. He turned quiet, his happy face now sallow. By the time they arrived at Grand Cayman three days later, his hands were three times their normal size and the rest of Dave had seemed to shrink. "Is he okay?" her daughter whispered, as he disembarked.

Dave was not okay. Health care on Grand Cayman was, in a word, expensive. They had already cashed out most of their money from their RRSPs, initially to pay for the navigational system, not to mention diesel fuel, and soon, they spent a great deal more getting Dave's diagnosis, which, as Pat suspected, was rheumatoid arthritis. Pat knew the condition meant Dave could eventually end up in a wheelchair. After a year on Grand Cayman, the unexpected reality of ill health meant their plan to sail to the Galapagos Islands had reached a sad conclusion. It was time to dock *H&E Hope*.

They hired a captain and crew to take the boat, with them onboard, to Sarasota, Florida, for repairs, storage, and eventual sale. By now, their savings had dwindled, and what remained paid for the docking space. Once in Florida, with the crew paid and the boat safely ensconced, they rented a U-Haul and began plan B, with a focus on the central mountains of Mexico and Pat's big sister.

Taking the scenic route through New Orleans and Texas to San Miguel de Allende, Pat and Dave arrived at her sister's two-bedroom apartment in the middle of the night on September 20, 2014.

Pat's sister was a social butterfly in a thriving community of immigrants. She lived upstairs. Pat and Dave settled on the main floor, slowly acclimating to the breathy mountain air and the Spanish language, which neither spoke, at least not enough for a conversation.

As Dave's life narrowed, so, too, did Pat's. His hands burned. Pat helped him shower. She held his coffee cup to his lips. He hated this new dependency, but being Dave, he was patient. Pat got him an appointment with a rheumatologist who prescribed new medication, and his hands slowly settled down. Pat wanted Dave to see a heart specialist because, after two years of living at sea level, they were now at a high altitude, and she worried about the impact on his heart.

There was one huge stress relief. Mexico was wonderfully affordable. They paid $400 a month for their share of the apartment on a dirt road in a neighbourhood populated by locals, with laundry machines in the outdoor garden.

The apartment had a galley kitchen, which reminded them of cooking on the *H&E Hope*. As his hands healed, Dave wanted a project. He loved the painted tiles he saw in the marketplace in happy shades of orange and pink, and he got the landlord's permission to layer them across the countertop.

They had a new routine, with Pat puttering in the kitchen every morning, making him coffee and toast, while he stayed in bed a bit longer, enjoying the early morning warmth of the sunlight filtering into the room.

Two months after they arrived, on November 8, Pat slipped out of bed, letting Dave sleep. He was quiet, facing the window, away from her. She went to the kitchen. Made coffee and fried up a few slices of bacon on the old stovetop. Dood, their dog, walked into the kitchen, stared at her, left the room, and came back again, and again, watching her with sober eyes. Dave's bacon sandwich ready, Pat walked back to their room. He was in the exact same position as when she left. His eyes were closed. Pat touched his shoulder. In that beautiful sunshine, Dave was gone.

She pulled up a chair, and facing his body, she spoke words of love. She reminded him of their adventures while sailing down the American coast, before the trip went awry, and she asked him to forgive her for not getting him an appointment with a Mexican cardiologist, even though she had tried.

And then reality hit. Sobbing, she called her sister, and in that moment their childhood roles re-emerged, Pat the little sister asking for help. Her sister knew a local physician, and he came to their home later that day to make an official declaration of death. The body would have to be cremated within 24 hours, the doctor told her sister, in a language that Pat could not speak.

Dave was taken away. In the first few days, Pat stayed in their bedroom. She could not physically step outside the front door into the sun and the noisy abundance of street life. Her mind was heavy with a grief that enveloped her like a shroud.

Dood must have known.

The next few weeks were a blur. The dog stayed with her sister, while Pat flew to Sarasota. She sold the $200,000 boat for $40,000, the best deal she could get, and flew back to Mexico, planning to settle there, but nothing felt right. She couldn't speak Spanish nor did she fit in with her sister's crowd.

Everything pointed in one direction. Home. She had no idea what awaited.

DEPRIVATION FACTS

Inspired by the material deprivation index offered by Food Banks Canada, the National Institute on Ageing used a similar approach focused on those aged 50 and older. Examining the ability to pay for certain necessities, such as healthy food, transportation, or winter boots, it created a deprivation index that gives a much different perspective on the affordability of life in 2024 when compared to Canada's official poverty numbers.

- Among those aged 65 and older, 14 percent lived in deprivation, more than double Canada's official poverty rate, which at the time was 6 percent. The 2025 figure was 5 percent.
- One in five Canadians aged 50 and older experience a poverty-level standard of living.
- Among the most vulnerable are those in poor health, women, renters, and single-person households.

CHAPTER TEN

The Warning

When it comes to the gender pension gap in Canada, we have good news, bad news, and caveats.

Over the last 50 years, retirement income has increased for many Canadians. Old Age Security, for example, was indexed to inflation in the early 1970s. So was the Guaranteed Income Supplement.

In 1976, 34.3 percent of women aged 65 and older were defined as low income (after paying taxes) compared to 17.5 in 2022. This is a striking improvement, but it still accounts for some 700,000 women in 2022, a number which will be higher today.

Seemingly endless streams of data on poverty, low income, or median income are collected and analyzed by Statistics Canada. A 2024 analysis goes deep into comparative detail on the financial status of women, but this line sums it up: "Overall, older women had lower income, higher low-income and poverty rates, and relied more on government transfers than older men."

Without taking readers into that abyss of definitions, here is an illustrative point captured by the report and my follow-up questions to Statistics Canada. In 2022, the median income (after tax) for male and female Canadians aged 65 and older was $32,000. The average older man received $38,700 per year. As for the average older woman? She lived on $28,600. It was worse for women who are racialized and women who immigrated later in life.

For those who claim the official poverty rate shows all is well among older Canadians, imagine living on that income and paying $2,400 a month in rent (or even $2,000) *and* eating. Beware of those citing averages to claim sweeping success. Nuances tell a much different story.

Dr. Elizabeth Shilton, a legal scholar, author, and pension expert, highlighted this disconnect in her damning 2024 report on Canada's gender pension gap for the Ontario Pay Equity Office (PEO).

"Canada has one of the best retirement income systems in the world," Dr. Shilton wrote. "But all Canadians do not benefit equally from the system. Masked by the good-news data is a substantial and persistent gender pension gap."

Which, naturally, brings us to women, old and young, given Canada's immutable pension gap. The contrast in retirement income between men and women, Shilton's report said, has not changed since 1976 when Canada's first "meaningful" statistics were collected.

This prolonged inequity is perplexing since women are increasingly educated and employed; the reasons for the gender pension gap, today and in the future, remain locked in the past.

The History

In the 1960s, *Mad Men* culture and all its Y chromosomes dominated in ways that most cannot comprehend today, even if certain American politicians are trying to resurrect that way of life.

That decade soon entered a period of sweeping societal change, upturned by the young, but in the early years, the big issues focused on established workers, mostly men who rightly demanded protections for their pensions. While those workers achieved some success, retirement pensions are to this day built on a philosophy defined in the late 1800s.

By men for men. But mostly for companies that needed committed workers.

For those who are pension-curious, Dr. Shilton's book, *Empty Promises: Why Workplace Pension Law Doesn't Deliver Pensions*, offers a fascinating dissemination on the reasons Canada's private workplace pensions are failing so many. On the foundational point of their original purpose, she explains:

> Canada's private workplace pension system was not designed to produce adequate, predictable, and secure pensions for workers. It was designed to meet the business needs of employers. For much of the 20th century, pension plans functioned as valuable human-resource management tools for employers whose business model demanded a stable workforce of loyal well-trained employees. They assisted enterprises to attract career-minded employees, to retain them throughout their productive working lives, to influence their workplace behaviour, and

> to ease them out the door when they became too old to be productive.

Canada's first company pension launched in 1874, offered to management at the Grand Trunk Railway. Employee pensions arrived later. During this period of rapid industrial expansion, businesses competed hard for workers, and pensions helped buy loyalty. As Dr. Shilton noted in an interview, the railroads, banks, and insurance companies that fostered the development of private pensions held all the power. Remarkably, there were no regulations protecting a worker's pension from an employer's whims.

"You could lose every penny of your pension if you were fired the day before you hit retirement age," she said. "A lot of the pensions were fundamentally discretionary. If you changed your job midstream, you would lose your pension."

Demand for reform grew. The first province to act, Ontario, passed the Pensions Benefits Act of 1962–63, far-reaching legislation that planned to mandate pensions in *all* workplaces with more than 15 employees, Shilton's book said. Imagine, today, the benefit of near universal workplace pensions.

Alas, it was not to be. The legislation would not come into force until January 1, 1965, and before the clock ran out, the business lobby won the support of political leaders who soon repealed the Act.

While Ontario successfully killed these life-enhancing reforms, it compromised with legislation that enshrined some protection for workers, placing limits on free-wheeling corporate control over pensions and employees' lives. Political leaders were later lauded for the Pension Benefits Act of 1965, which made Ontario the first Canadian province to regulate these workplace benefits. Its meagre half measures were copied by others.

In the background of that debate was the demand for a public pension, a partnership between federal and provincial governments. Despite calls for a gold standard public plan that would replace as much as 70 percent of a worker's earlier income, Ontario politicians voted for a lesser amount, arguing that private workplace plans would bridge the retirement income gap (and perpetuate worker loyalty). Another win for the business lobby.

Instead of replacing a substantial portion of a retiree's earlier income, the CPP covers only 25 percent. Changes that began in 2019 will eventually lead to a 33 percent wage replacement but won't be fully realized until 2059, when today's 25-year-olds retire.

In the 1960s, the public pension was deemed mandatory. This was a win accompanied by the loss of substantial wage replacement. To justify such a small payout, the government said the CPP would serve to enhance the superior workplace pension, a decision that might have made sense if companies were required to offer a workplace pension, which they were not.

It is worth acknowledging that during the great pension debate, married women were seen as dependent on their husbands. Politicians (men) raised their voices to protect family sanctity by suggesting that a housewife should not be incentivized to join the workforce with the lure of a pension. Instead, a wife would benefit from her husband's workplace pension, and if he died, she would receive a (smaller) CPP survivor's benefit. As Shilton's PEO report explains:

> Policy makers responsible for the design of Canada's retirement income were not oblivious or indifferent to gender, they nevertheless constructed and maintained a system designed to deliver its best rewards

> for male pattern employment. Lawmakers reasoned that while homemaking women were not likely to accumulate their own pension credits, they would nevertheless benefit from improved pensions for workers. Women who had been supported by their husbands' wages would continue to be supported by their husbands' pensions once those husbands retired. If their husbands predeceased them, the preferred solution built into the CPP from the outset was the smaller survivor pension for dependents of contributors.

For all their labour raising children, supporting husbands, and running households like the small businesses that they were, politicians and CPP's founding fathers chose a reduced survivor's pension for women who, statistically, would outlive their husbands by many years.

The CPP did allow working women — often single and without children — to pay into the public pension system. As Dr. Shilton notes in an interview, those women only benefitted if their contributions continued over a long and uninterrupted career. Private workplace pensions were a different matter. Much like today, some got a pension, while others did not. As always, the higher an employee's salary, the better the pension. And we know how that worked out.

Survivors' pensions were a "partial solution," the PEO report says, but for many years these options ignored divorced women or those living in same-sex relationships, "all of whom gained little" from pension structures designed for the careers of men.

But to paraphrase 1964 Dylan, times were a-changin'. As feminists rallied for economic and reproductive independence, women increasingly found employment outside the home. The way women viewed themselves, their worth, and their opportunities for a life of their choosing transformed, no longer dictated by husbands and tradition.

In hindsight, it is worth noting that those changes, wonderful, empowering, and life-saving, meant many women spent more hours working at a job *and* at home. This is called an unanticipated outcome. The new workload affected the gender pension gap with its limiting impact on career advancement among exhausted female employees.

It is hard to do it all. Back in the day, young men embraced the free love movement but were less keen on the result, laundry and kids, a trend that while statistically declining — at least by men self-reporting — still exists to this day.

And so, the fight for equality carried on, for decades.

Survivor benefits for couples in same-sex relationships were not provided until 2000 and were only given to those whose partners had died in a narrow window of time, starting in 1998. It took another nine years for a Supreme Court of Canada decision to ensure that CPP gave survivor benefits to those whose same-sex partners had died prior to that cut-off date.

In the 1970s, as two-income households became increasingly common, women's advocates pushed for changes to the public pension. Some improvements helped, such as pension credit splitting during a divorce or the exclusion of low-earning periods for mothers who left work to stay at home with children.

Rather than additional policy change that would support female-pattern employment, politicians claimed that pension equality would come from equal wages. But in the 1980s, as the PEO report points out, the momentum of women's earning power slowed and the gender wage gap did not disappear.

If they are still alive, the women who fought for those changes are now in their 70s, 80s, and 90s. Some believe those women are the last to live through the gender pension gap. According to Dr. Shilton, they are wrong.

The Motherhood Penalty

In 2021, the federal government announced a plan for $10-a-day child care helping provinces implement the programs; Quebec had long had such a program.

British Columbia signed on first with a projected annual savings (estimated by the feds) of $10,800 for full-time child care of a young child. Programs in Nunavut and Alberta promised the highest maximum savings, at $16,000 and $13,000 respectively. Ontario came on board with future savings estimated at as much as $10,000. Unfortunately, half of Canada's provinces were not expected to reach these targets in 2026 as planned, including Ontario, Alberta, B.C., and Nunavut.

Still, this is public policy that has the potential to change lives. It can enrich young children whose brains embrace the joy of learning new words, art, and music. It saves families thousands of dollars in child-care costs. And it increases labour market participation of mothers with young children, whether married or single.

Affordable child care that allows women to continue working is also good for finances in old age. But, as many new mothers discover, a career after parental leave doesn't mean a return to the high-performance track.

Early analysis on trends in female employment make this a good place to introduce the Financial Accountability Office of Ontario. Established in 2013, the FAO is mandated to provide independent analysis on provincial finances, budgets, and economics. In 2023, it analyzed the impact of $10-a-day child care and the labour force participation of women. Its report concluded that "large gaps remain in labour market participation and outcomes between men and women." Most interesting were the FAO's fresh facts on the "motherhood earnings penalty," otherwise known as the motherhood penalty. Examining working Ontarian mothers in two cohorts (2003 and 2014), the FAO found that after having a child, it took women up to four years to return to their pre-childbirth earnings.

Since the gender wage gap is connected to lifelong inequities, women on average start their careers with near pay parity. Women under the age of 25 have the smallest wage gap, making 95 cents for every dollar earned by men in the same age group. But it doesn't last.

Between the ages of 25 and 54, generally when women are immersed in parenting, they make 87 cents for every dollar earned by a man in the same age cohort. And while some are dismissive of such statistics, saying the difference in hourly wages or annual pay is due to vastly different job categories, the FAO found that only two cents of that 13-cent wage gap is related to the *type* of job a woman holds.

Mostly, wages are impacted by tradition. The report explains:

> The larger wage gap at older ages reflects in part the impact of caretaking responsibilities which tend to increase with age and fall predominantly on women. Core-age women are more likely to take time away from the labour market to raise children or attend to family responsibilities, leading to employment

> disruptions at a time in their career when their labour market attachment would otherwise be the strongest.
>
> These caregiving responsibilities can impede women's ability to put in long hours that are needed to secure promotions in certain industries, develop networks to facilitate movement to higher paying jobs, as well as create incentives for selecting lower-paying jobs with limited hour requirements.

Recognition of the motherhood penalty matters. It can take a toll spiritually, physically, and financially, this struggle to pursue a career while shouldering responsibility for collecting children from daycare, cooking dinner, checking homework, getting kids out the door for evening sports, and reading bedtime stories, all the while keeping a clean-ish house.

Many women settle for lesser jobs. Others grind through the years. Some get divorced. Eventually, a smaller income leads to a diminished pension and an RRSP that can never be maxed out.

The Good News

In 2023, Canada had 20.2 million actively working adults. Less than half, some seven million men and women, paid into a private workplace pension. This means 13 million did not. (For clarity, we are talking about company pensions, not the public CPP.)

Despite a long-term decline in workplace pensions, overall membership ticked upward in 2023: 9.6 million adult women worked in 2023, and 3.7 million paid into a workplace pension; of the 10.6 million men who worked, 3.5 million paid into a workplace pension. The lower numbers for men are due, in no small part, to a 20-year decline in good union jobs and the rise of new employers that don't offer a workplace pension. Nobody benefits from that trend.

The growth of women's membership in private pension plans is undeniably excellent and noteworthy, but it does not negate the reality that many women won't retire with the highest possible payments due to the motherhood penalty's impact on salary and career ascent. Besides, not all pensions are equal.

To engage in a little anthropomorphism of pension plans, the defined benefit plans are the podium superstars, the Christine Sinclairs or Hayley Wickenheisers, so to speak, of retirement income vehicles. The defined contribution plans, well, they're playing on the farm team, pretty good but not badass, as the kids say. Two-thirds of the 7.2 million workers paying into a pension plan in 2023 had a defined benefit pension.

That is roughly 4.8 million very lucky people, with women accounting for a little more than half; many work in the public sector, as bureaucrats, teachers, nurses, municipal workers, or office staff. The list is almost endless. (Given the hiring spree in federal government jobs in recent years, some jobs now risk layoffs.) The rise in public sector jobs is excellent news, highlighting women's success in education and professional achievements.

Less compelling is the fact that the *proportion* of all Canadian workers paying into any type of workplace pension plan declined to 37.7 percent in 2023 from 39.7 in 2020. In the late 1970s, *more than 50 percent* of Canadian workers (mostly men) had a workplace pension. Those retired workers are counted in today's data on the overall financial well-being of older adults; future cohorts will not be so blessed.

And to drill home the not-so-great news, proportionally speaking, 62.3 percent of Canada's 20 million workers in 2023 were not paying into any workplace pension, which means, caveats aside, most workers do not have one.

For policy-makers focused on the future, this is wildly problematic.

Of course, not everyone needs a private pension. Those with wealth won't miss it. And many high-paid professionals can save enough to manage a comfortable retirement, despite the adage that says the more you earn, the more you spend.

Having acknowledged those blessed with public service jobs (at least those not impacted by budget cuts) and the lucrative salaries of some who are pension-free, it seems fair to state the obvious: A great many people with no workplace pension can barely pay their mortgage or rent, let alone invest in RRSPs. Many Canadians aged 50 and older have less than $5,000 in savings.

But retirement planning? If you're lucky enough to stay healthy, the best protection against old-age poverty might be lifelong employment. In other words, carry on.

The "C" Jobs

All this good news complicated by reality feels a bit twisted, like a statistical narcissism that delights in gaslighting.

Increasingly, women are moving into traditionally male zones: science, technology, engineering, and mathematics — STEM jobs that pay well, offer upward mobility, and can be fully or partially remote, supporting work-life balance.

Recognizing this trend, schools and parents emphasize STEM studies. It has been said by some educators that anyone can learn high-level math, which truly would be a glorious thing. And yet the FAO reports that more women than men still join non-STEM employment or lower-paid STEM jobs in health care, education, and social and behavioural sciences.

"While educational attainment has increased significantly for women," the FAO report on women's labour said, "certain key differences in the field of study chosen by men and women may impact lifelong earnings potential. In 2020, women significantly outnumbered men in health, education, social and behavioral sciences and law fields, while men outnumbered women in science, technology, engineering, and mathematics (STEM) fields that have significantly higher income potential."

At the Pay Equity Office of Ontario, Kadie Philp, commissioner and chief administrative officer, takes these observations a step further. "Women are still clustered in what we call 'the Cs,' the clerical, the cashier, the care worker," Philp says. "They are clustered in jobs that are still undervalued and underpaid. We put more weight on, say, a firefighter who's providing an essential life-saving service than we do a nurse in Emerg who is also providing an essential life-saving service." Emergency department nurses are often assaulted by patients, sometimes severely, so they face danger of a different kind than a firefighter.

The disconnect in the way jobs are valued, Philp says, ultimately leads to lower retirement income for women.

In the early stage of a career, most of us do not consider the long-term impact of our choices. It doesn't hit home until decades later when the retirement math doesn't add up.

The Advice

Dr. Tammy Schirle, the Wilfrid Laurier professor and economist who calls herself a "feminist and fiscalist," has considered the cost of divorce on a woman's financial longevity.

It can be profound.

"If you're thinking about somebody who is currently retired," Schirle says, "they may have been divorced long before their retirement. And if they had any children, they would have made sacrifices to their career to do that child-rearing.

"They took time away from work while they were still married to take care of kids, and that has a long-term penalty that we're getting really good at measuring now. For women who have kids and go back to work, they're looking at earning 30 to 40 percent less than they would have if they hadn't had kids. And that just comes with taking on the jobs that allow for flexibility to deal with all the child care, soccer, sick kids, all that stuff. So, you're looking at a career where you have lower earnings.

"While you're married, that's fine. You can think about negotiating that kind of work between you and your spouse. But upon divorce, it's not clear how well that gets accounted for in terms of the impact on your retirement income down the road."

What is typically not built into a divorce agreement or asset splitting is the impact of parenting on a woman's lower earnings when she eventually retires.

"She's never going to fully recover from that later in her career. And that's going to be built into her own Canada Pension Plan and any other savings that she has available for retirement," Schirle says.

"This is where I think many women have developed the incentive or recognition that having an income and pension of your own is really important because you can't really build that into a flawless marriage contract."

And so, from a feminist economist, here is a bit of wisdom for today's young women to prepare for life 40 years hence.

"I think," says Schirle, "it would be fair to say that when you are talking about both men and women, young people in the labour market today, if you don't get into a public service job, it's going to be very, very difficult to find the type of secure retirement income that you might underappreciate when you're young but will certainly become important when you're older.

"The challenge for women is higher, to the extent that any time taken away for the caregiving of children is going to impact their career and further impact their ability to put away those retirement savings.

"It is really important for young women to first try to find a job that offers those type of benefits. But when you can, you also need to *make sure you have a partner who's going to share in family responsibilities*, to minimize the penalty to your own career, rather than taking on the full cost yourself."

A warning for women entering the job market — and the dating apps.

CHAPTER ELEVEN

Pat

Mexico offered a cheap existence, but Pat could not stay. Without Dave, it was not home and the painted tiles from the marketplace that he had so happily added to the kitchen counter mocked her with their joyous shades of orange and pink.

In early 2015, Pat returned to Canada and soon realized that most of her friends had scattered, seeking their own dream retirements after cashing out of the real estate market. They assumed, perhaps, that home values had reached an all-time high, though the ascent had just begun.

Alone, Pat felt numb. The grey slush of winter matched her mood.

She was almost 65 years old and had to start over, yet again. The first time, after her divorce, it was exciting to create a new life. This time, well, her heart hurt. And she had to figure out how to survive the remainder of her days. When you worry about spending money to eat, the length of one's existence takes on new significance.

In a move that made sense in the haze of that first year, Pat bought herself a $22,000 mobile home from what was left of the $40,000 from the boat. She found it at a trailer park outside Peterborough, Ontario, near Pigeon Lake, and considered moving it to a park in Prince Edward County but after visiting, it seemed too high end with so many $200,000 mobile homes. "It was a hoity-toity trailer park," she'd say, laughing.

Pat decided to stay at the Pigeon Lake trailer park, a more affordable existence but it closed for six months during the cold season. Pat figured she could find a cheap place to stay during the winter. She could not. But in the first warm months, Pat grew to love her little trailer. It looked like a tiny house, just 12 feet long with an arched roof and a white picket fence on the front deck. She had a patch of grass, a firepit, and a place to park an ancient Toyota Corolla bought on the cheap.

Pat built herself a nest here. In the summer, amidst the rolling green of the Ontario countryside, the idea of colour started to captivate her. She painted the inside walls of her trailer yellow and blue, an ode to French Provincial decor. As she worked, Pat talked to Dave, asking his thoughts, telling him she wished they were painting together.

Outside, she planted a shrub and a few small hydrangeas in blue and yellow. Physical labour felt good. At night, she fell into a deep sleep. Maybe her body craved the work and rest, because during that little stretch of time, Pat stopped feeling quite so sorry for herself and just grieved the loss of her man. Alone, her thoughts became a reassuring mantra: "You're okay. You'll figure it out. Things always get better."

As summer waned, Pat decided she needed to meet new people and make a friend or two. After so many days spent alone, starting a conversation with actual humans seemed intimidating. It's hard to make new friends after a certain age, especially when most are settled into routines with people they have known for years. Pat heard about a local coffee meet-up in a Peterborough seniors' centre and decided to go. As she walked toward the door, she felt shaky, as if at a grown-up version of the first day at school; always the public health nurse, she told herself it's good for the brain to do hard things. She stood back for a bit, surveying the room and saw three women her age at a table. She took a breath, walked over, asked if she could join. Two glanced her way and continued their conversation. One smiled at Pat, so she sat down, and they started chatting about the community, the weather, the usual conversation openers. Pat explained that she had just moved to Peterborough.

"Where do you live?" the woman asked politely.

"In the Pigeon Lake trailer park," Pat said.

"Oh," said the woman and turned back to her friends.

For a moment, Pat sat in silence. She stood up and walked away.

It was in the blur of those lonely years that she decided to find a new relationship through online dating. The problem was her energy didn't match the yellow on her trailer walls and certainly not Dave's kitchen tiles. Pat knew she wasn't exactly a vision of exuberance, but she loved conversation with interesting men.

If her age didn't dampen male enthusiasm, at least with one fussbudget old guy who wanted someone younger, she soon realized her finances did. In the mature dating scene, impoverishment was a non-negotiable, and Pat concluded that men with a decent retirement income didn't want a woman who had no assets.

Some days Pat felt like she was in a hole sinking. She didn't like the helplessness of self-pity. Nor did she enjoy this new focus on pure survival, life without a bigger plan. Pat's natural default was to be an organizer, always with a project on the go. After the harshness of that one date, she withdrew, almost in shame for not knowing her apparent place as a lovely woman in her late 60s. She consoled herself with thoughts of Dave, the man her "List of Conditions" for a relationship had manifested all those years ago. Her hope for new love was over, with nothing to fill the space.

Late at night, as Pat sat outside her trailer, staring at the sparkling summer sky, she asked the universe to give her life purpose, something new, something she had never imagined.

Still, she had to figure out the present.

Short-term rentals through the last few winters cost more than she could afford, sending her into debt. She might need to give up her sweet trailer and find a permanent place to live in a traditional version of low-income housing. She toured rooming houses with shared washrooms; after meeting the gaze of grizzled male tenants, she decided to keep looking and eventually grew so distressed at the cost of apartments that she looked up the address for the municipal office that managed Peterborough's subsidized housing.

Pat drove to the office and stood in line. It did not feel like she, a woman who once sailed with the Bronte Harbour Yacht Club, belonged here, asking for a rent-geared-to-income apartment. But she did.

When it was her turn at the counter, Pat spoke to the woman behind the window who, she noticed, did not look in her direction, not once. Staring at her computer, the worker pushed a piece of paper, an application, toward Pat. "Fill this out," she said, as if talking to her desktop. If Pat had immediately walked to a nearby bank and robbed it at gunpoint, the housing worker could not have provided a description to police because her eyes did not once turn toward Pat's presence.

Pat folded the application neatly and put it in her purse. She turned and walked out, the room blurred. She didn't see the others waiting in line. Her energy was focused on getting to her car in the parking lot. And there it was, a 20-year-old Toyota Corolla. Grey with rust around the doors and a few hundred thousand kilometres on the odometer, but it was reliable and waiting. Pat opened the door, sat down, and, gripping the steering wheel, started sobbing. She stayed, head down, for a long time.

Eventually, Pat gave up on finding anything affordable in Ontario and spent money on an airplane ticket to British Columbia to winter with her sister. She had returned from Mexico to deal with a health problem that would soon be diagnosed as melanoma and ultimately end quite peacefully through medical assistance in dying.

Her sister had rented a 500-square-foot one-bedroom apartment in North Saanich, about 25 kilometres outside Victoria, on Vancouver Island. The front door opened to the living room, with a small coffee table, two chairs, and a grey sofa. The wall on the right side had floor-to-ceiling shelves filled with books.

Pat's sister offered a dresser drawer and the couch, which luckily was long enough to hold her five-foot-nine frame. It was solid, too, which was good for Pat's back. These are all considerations.

With older sibling energy, Pat's sister told her to forget men, especially relationships, declaring those days over. At this age, men want a hearse, a nurse, or a purse, she'd say, laughing. She challenged Pat to adapt to life as a single woman, even explaining the sexual pleasures to be found in the bathtub from a steady stream of warm water and a pulsating faucet. Pat was impressed with her sister's revelations, but none of the options presented worked for her, including the most traditional. She still wanted a man, although at this point she mostly wanted to survive.

Late one night, on her sister's computer, Pat scrolled through housing options and discovered women living in their cars, mainly in the southern U.S. where winters are survivable. She read their Facebook posts about safety and cleanliness. Women like to stay presentable. She could see herself in their stories. This was the answer!

Next year, after the trailer park closed, she would drive to Florida and live there as a nomad, like the others. It was an immediate relief, having a plan, even if it scared her. When she explained it to her sister the next day, Pat wept. Her sister hugged her. It was the first time since just after Dave died that she'd felt the kindness of human touch.

That evening, Pat returned to the Facebook site. It was loaded with revelations, such as how to accurately pee into a cup-like device at 3 a.m. As she scrolled further, reaching deep into the stories women shared, Pat felt sick. All the jobs juggled and taxes paid, all the energy expended on caring for husbands while raising the next generation of taxpayers, and in the end, women are discarded.

She spent most of the night awake. From the car-life scare came a new idea: communal living. It was a better solution, and, she thought, it must be more affordable. From the couch in Victoria, Pat googled the cost of a four-bedroom rental in Peterborough and realized that with the right roommates, rent would be manageable. Her brain shifted from despair into thinking mode. Pat was a problem solver, and it wasn't long before she created a Facebook group and posted a public message about her impossible Canadian housing search. "Am I the only woman in this predicament? Is anyone else living this way?"

If it turned out the way she hoped, Pat would find three roommates for a rental and close the Facebook site. If nothing else, Pat figured she'd find a few women to chat with online and lessen her loneliness.

The following morning, awakening later than usual, she made a cup of tea and logged on to her profile. Ten messages awaited. All from women who said they were in the same position. The next day she had another 50 messages. Notifications kept arriving. By the end of the month, there were 200 detailed responses. So many women, older women, living on the edge of financial distress. Some had secretly lived in cars, unbeknownst to their families. Many were ashamed.

Pat's message offered a place to connect with others who understood, and suddenly the realization arrived.

The plea she had made to the universe months earlier, outside her trailer under the open sky, that big ask for a new purpose in life, well, it finally made its way home.

THE WOMEN'S HEALTH FACTS

- Between 1997 and 2000, eight of the ten prescriptions drugs withdrawn from the U.S. market posed greater health risks for women than for men.
- Heart disease and stroke are the leading causes of premature death for women in Canada.
- Almost two-thirds of people aged 65 and older living with Alzheimer's disease are women.
- Women provide two-thirds of dementia care to family members.

CHAPTER TWELVE

The Doctor

It has been decades now since Dr. Paula Rochon worked as a geriatrician in a Toronto long-term care home with so many female residents that dining-room gatherings offered visual proof of the actuarial claim that women outlive men.

In Dr. Rochon's family, it was her grandfather who had longevity. He was an eternal optimist, always in motion, and lived almost to the age of 103. The way he embraced life was an inspiration for the young physician choosing her specialty. She explored the many possibilities. Early in medical school, the idea of a rural family practice intrigued her. As the world opened, so did her interest in specialties — internal medicine or endocrinology and infertility.

The right conversation can open the mind to new possibilities, and a meeting with a geriatrician introduced Dr. Rochon to a practice she had not contemplated. She envisioned her grandfather, a man who was the definition of lifelong enthusiasm, and realized that geriatrics offered a fresh perspective, new ideas on the act of growing old. It also provided tangible ways to make a difference.

"In geriatrics, you could hear their stories, you could understand what their particular problems were," Dr. Rochon says. "You could help people have the resources they need or develop strategies that might be helpful or think about medications that might be better for them. You were helping them achieve what they wanted to achieve."

After completing geriatric training in Toronto hospitals during the early 1990s, Dr. Rochon went to the United Kingdom for advanced research training before earning a master's of public health at Harvard School of Public Health in Cambridge, Massachusetts, where one of her first papers examined studies on arthritis and concluded that despite its significant risk among older adults, research primarily examined the bodies of young people.

Returning to Toronto with a public health background added to her specialty in geriatrics, Dr. Rochon began working in the nursing home where a great many women lived. It was there that she recognized a trend. Older women did not always respond to pharmaceutical treatments as predicted, which sometimes led to adverse drug effects. The reasons for this, Dr. Rochon says, are multifactorial but are related, at least in part, to body composition, hormones, or slower clearance from the system.

Some drug doses could cause low blood pressure, possibly leading to unsteady gait and, potentially, falls that might shatter fragile bones. Other drugs, including antipsychotics, potentially led to confusion.

In the long-term care home, Dr. Rochon's immediate concern focused on women who were overwhelmed by certain medications. When she tried to scale back the potency of prescriptions, she discovered that drug companies did not consistently make pills in sufficiently small doses better suited to the sensitivities of older people, especially women. So, as pharmacists split pills into smaller pieces for her patients, Dr. Rochon explored the medical literature, looking for details on the people that researchers examined as part of their studies. In doing so, she once again encountered the biases of sex and age.

Shortly after she published papers on pill splitting for the best dose among older patients, pharmaceutical reps started sending her splitting devices to help residents get smaller doses, but to Dr. Rochon, the solution was complex.

"It made me look at 'Why?'" she says.

Like others who were shining a female-centric lens on medical care, Dr. Rochon questioned the design of clinical trials that used mostly younger men as subjects, a historical approach that led to a mismatch between the evidence in academic papers and the real world. There was no requirement, she wrote, that clinical trials include women, nor were trials required to examine older people even though age-related conditions left them most at risk.

Throughout much of the 20th century, clinical trials did not generally study women. Of any age. Most research used men or (male) mice. Since older women often react differently to treatments than their male peers, the need for research on age and sex differences became increasingly clear.

"Just simplistically to me, it didn't make sense," Rochon says. "The people that are using the drugs, those who might be more vulnerable, aren't being studied."

The answers she sought led to an unexpected path, away from front-line geriatrics to research with a wider perspective using population-level data to explore an emerging concept: public health and aging women.

And so, the doctor became a scientist too. Published in academic journals, her work deconstructed sex and age bias in pharmaceutical research, inspired by her initial front-line observations that older people, mostly women, react differently to medications and doses, often with sensitivities to the most basic drugs. Older adults, especially women, were frequently underrepresented in studies on treatments for cardiovascular disease, even though there is a higher incidence with age.

Earlier research, if it examined older adults at all, looked at men and women as if there were no differences. Women's bodies are uniquely complex, older women's bodies are different than younger women's bodies, and older women are different than older men.

The knowledge gaps persist, but as the work of Dr. Rochon and other scientists shows, research data should explore the nuances of sex and age so any differences or similarities are recognized. These variances can also intersect with race and socio-economic status. All have the potential to play a significant role in our health, as does ageism, the gender pension gap, and the lack of affordable housing that includes health and social supports, as Dr. Rochon's work later exposed.

All of these discoveries, all of her training, built toward 2021 when Dr. Rochon founded the Women's Age Lab within Women's College Hospital in downtown Toronto. Internationally, the Women's Age Lab appears to be the only such research lab focused primarily on the health and well-being of older women. Dr. Rochon says she has searched globally for another such entity but is unable to find one. She introduces Women's Age Lab as one of a kind. "I keep saying that, and no one corrects me," she says, laughing.

Before we talk about research emerging from Women's Age Lab, it helps to understand, at least in part, how women were excluded from North American clinical trials.

One of the challenges of research that included women was the devastating outcome of the thalidomide drug, prescribed to pregnant women in the late 1950s and early 1960s to limit nausea. If taken early in pregnancy, it risked altering the development of the embryos, leading to shortened limbs along with losses in hearing and eyesight, facial paralysis, and issues with internal organs. Globally, including Canada, it is estimated that more than 10,000 babies were affected by the drug. It was not approved for use in America, but its impact did not go unnoticed.

The U.S. National Institutes of Health (NIH) has said that concerns about drug-related incidents, particularly after thalidomide's harm was exposed, led to the 1977 Food and Drug Administration policy that banned all premenopausal women in the U.S. from taking part in phase I and early phase II drug trials: "The policy was broad and recommended excluding even women who used contraception, who were single, or whose husbands were vasectomized," according to the NIH "History of Women's Participation in Clinical Research."

"Excluding women from early stages of drug trials led to a shortage of data on how drugs affect women," the NIH document said. "Many people believed that individual women should be allowed to choose whether to take the risk of participating in research. For example, activists protested the exclusion of women from trials of HIV drugs."

Another problem predated thalidomide, though its impact did not appear until the late 1960s. "In 1938, DES, a synthetic hormone prescribed to an estimated 200,000 to 400,000 Canadian women to prevent miscarriages, was found 30 years later to have harmful effects on their daughters; reducing fertility and causing adenocarcinoma (cancer) of the vagina," author Alla Yakerson wrote in the *International Journal for Equity in Health*. "Following the thalidomide and DES disasters, protective regulations directed towards women of child-bearing years became implemented."

In the 1980s, lower survival rates of women with AIDS led to a push among activists for access to experimental therapies, and once successful, Yakerson wrote, "women's advocacy continued with the recognition that clinical outcomes of medications must be evaluated on both sexes."

By the early 1990s, in the U.S. and Canada, there was growing pressure for inclusion of women in medical trials. The U.S. ban on premenopausal women in clinical trials funded through the NIH was lifted in 1993 when Congress wrote the NIH inclusion policy into federal law, ensuring that "women and minorities are included in all clinical research."

In 2019, the NIH adopted an "inclusion across lifespan" policy that required individuals under the age of 18 and older adults included in all research using humans as subjects, unless there are "scientific or ethical reasons" for exclusion.

But in early 2025, with a new federal government in power, the U.S. Department of Health and Human Services (HHS) issued directives against funding research related to diversity, inclusion, and equity. The NIH cancelled 2,100 research grants, according to Reuters. Lawsuits followed. Blistering court judgments ruled against the HHS directives; it is unclear if the court rulings will be upheld or for how long.

In Canada, it's different. Some 20 years ago, the Canadian Institutes of Health Research began integrating sex and gender-based analysis (SGBA) into the research grants it funds as part of its mandate. The CIHR says it has worked internationally to advance sex and gender science as a distinct field of study and as a necessary practice in health research.

In one example of biological sex differences, CIHR's Institute of Gender and Health (IGH) noted a study that looked at pain reduction in mice. Without delving into the science behind microglia functioning, let's just say that researchers were able to reduce pain in male mice but not in females. Conversely, females reaped the pain-lowering benefits of a different immune cell.

Cardiovascular disease is now noted for distinctions in relation to health outcomes after a heart attack by sex and gender. According to a report published by the IGH, a study led by Dr. Louise Pilote developed a gender index that allows researchers to measure sex and gender independently: The study found that "patients of both sexes who scored high on factors traditionally considered 'feminine' were more likely to have symptoms recur in the year after their initial cardiac event, compared to those who scored higher on masculine traits." What that means, the IGH report said, is that "personality traits and social roles typically assigned to or associated with women may increase the risk of negative outcomes in patients with cardiac disease."

In Canada, the IGH has rather relentlessly promoted the message that "sex and gender are critical components of rigorous and reproducible science." That strategy requires, according to IGH, "creativity and persistence to take sex and gender integration to the next level — from awareness to implementation."

Of course, the exclusion of women is not exclusive to medicine.

Crash-test dummies might be the most relatable example of bias, with potentially deadly results. In my interview with Dr. Rochon, she mentioned *Invisible Women* by Caroline Criado Perez, which said the dummies used to withstand car-crash testing are modelled after a man in the 50th height and weight percentile — not too big, not too small. If you are a man.

For women, that model is not just oversized, it is also incorrectly designed for the shape of a female body. Auto accident data, the book reports, shows that women are more likely than men to be injured or die. There are untold other examples that show the world of consumer design, movies, and even banknote images do not consider women.

Unless confronted with proof, most of us do not think about the impact of these biases, which is a circuitous way of bringing us back to the Women's Age Lab, where inequities and solutions are pretty much all they contemplate.

The research centre that Dr. Rochon created is on an upper floor of the Women's College Hospital building, just west of Bay Street in downtown Toronto. It is a national base for geriatricians, gerontologists, epidemiologists, and statistical analysts, all of whom focus on two combined subject areas: aging and women. Their explorations examine overarching themes — for women of all ages. These include better research for medical therapies such as drugs, promoting social connections to reduce loneliness, caregiving, and aging in the right place.

To explore the first theme — improved research for medical therapies — the Women's Age Lab reports underscore the challenges facing women as they advance through life.

"Women and older adults being excluded from clinical trials leads to a gap in the understanding of how drugs impact them," Rochon and her team wrote in a 2024 report called "Women at the Forefront of Aging in Canada."

"Older women have more chronic conditions than men and often have multiple chronic conditions. They are generally thought to use more medications and experience more adverse drug events.

"To this day, the collection and use of data disaggregated by sex, gender, and age is lagging, hindering the ability to fully understand the needs of older women and to create tailored interventions for them."

It seems fair to say that medical research, in many ways, has failed women throughout life, but the general lack of knowledge about older women's bodies and health can lead to problems that could be avoided or at least lessened. Given all the other challenges women face, this is extraordinarily unfair.

Women, more than men, are diagnosed with Alzheimer's disease. The reason why remains unanswered, though Dr. Rochon says research shows it is related in part to traditionally lower levels of physical activity and education among women. The potential for such late-life vulnerabilities, Dr. Rochon warns, is likely influenced by decisions made years in advance.

How many of us, she says, sat behind a desk during our career and never really committed to regular exercise? Or how many were so busy juggling work with family that there was no personal time for fitness?

A growing body of evidence shows that higher levels of physical activity can be associated with a reduced risk of Alzheimer's disease. "It is not to say that just because you're physically active, you're not going to have dementia, but these things all contribute," she says. "And if there are pieces you can do that might be helpful, we should be thinking about that. Especially as women."

Research can point the way, but politicians and policy-makers using that evidence could, if they choose, create tangible improvements in the lives of older women — including the housing needed to keep people connected to community.

That brings us to the Age Lab's second theme: housing and why it matters deeply in healthier aging. We will delve deeper in a later chapter, but for now it is worth noting that many of us do not consider the connection between an affordable home and health. Nor do we think about the value of housing that comes with home care and social supports.

Affordable community-based housing with those extra services can make a world of difference. While this may be endangered by the Trump administration's plans to cut some funding to Medicaid, the U.S. PACE program provides home care, bathing, grocery shopping, and housecleaning, and it is increasingly the model that Medicaid supports, instead of nursing homes. If America is doing it, why can't Canada?

As Dr. Rochon and her team wrote in the *Journal of the American Geriatrics Society*, innovative housing models can help older adults with affordability, health, loneliness, and isolation: "Poverty and loneliness are key factors to consider when exploring innovative resident-coordinated housing models, as lower pensions — if they have a pension at all — can be a barrier preventing older women from securing housing, ultimately reducing social connectedness and impeding aging-in-place."

It's worth exploring housing options earlier in life than later when in crisis mode. Some of those conversations are starting among friends, Rochon says, even if they are masked in lighthearted conversation.

"When we go out, people sort of jokingly talk about where they want to go, how they want to live, or buy properties to share together because it is starting to catch on that maybe women might outlive a spouse. At least according to statistics. So, who would they like to live with? Maybe it's companionship they want. And so how do they create an environment that is around the people they want to be around? It could be women, it could be men, it doesn't really matter; what is important is that it is the way they want to live," Dr. Rochon says. "People are starting to think about those things. You don't need to wait till you're 80 or 90 to start thinking about those conversations."

Here is some demographic context worth repeating: In Canada, where the 85-plus age group is the fastest-growing cohort, we still do not have a national aging strategy to address the public health threat that comes from loneliness and social isolation, with the troubling potential links to heart disease, depression, and dementia.

In 2021, the Commonwealth Fund Survey on Older Adults looked at 11 countries, including Canada, the U.K., and the United States. It concluded that social isolation is highest among older Canadians, particularly women and those living alone.

Older women, of all ethnicities, are among society's most invisible, and despite advocates' repeated calls for a national strategy on loneliness, the federal government has not acted. Yes, significant money flows through organizations that support small-scale and temporary community engagement grants. And lower levels of government may provide some programs for "seniors." But on this overarching issue — the precarious lives of older women — little has changed.

This is the fault line, where pioneers in the field of female-focused research stand on one side, and on the other are policy-makers with a different vision of compelling need. There are any number of advocacy groups writing reports on aging, but few are focused on the female experience, especially of women challenged by the debilitating trifecta of finances, housing, and isolation.

In a blunt summation of what awaits, Women's Age Lab warns, "If these gaps are not addressed, Canada risks failing a major part of its population and risks leaving older women behind."

For people of any age, the struggle to exist on a low income means energy is dedicated to survival instead of, say, exploring creative pursuits or enjoying the pleasures brought by a physically strong body and mind. None of this is new, but it is older women who go unnoticed, particularly by those who control the policies that improve the way society's most vulnerable live. What is unmeasured is unmanaged.

CHAPTER THIRTEEN

Elizabeth

Sometimes it's best to tuck away feelings, even the sweet kind that come with a lovely twinge.

It starts as a bit of excitement perhaps at seeing a certain man, but as she works through the idea of this attraction (wondering, "Why not me?"), Elizabeth is well practised at dimming that little joy, that particular spring in her vigorous step. Maybe it's not joy at all; maybe it's just curiosity. Oh, wait. Maybe it's not curiosity but just unexpected warmth toward a guy who gives good conversation, which, to be sure, is very appealing.

The analytical side of Elizabeth acknowledges the desire to be connected in a romantic way, to be loved, but after some consideration, she decides this feeling is just the young part of herself, the little girl who needs to feel protected and was simply raising her hand to be noticed. The truth is possibly more complicated. And it doesn't resolve with advancing years. Nor is it expected to in a society that disabuses older people of seeking physical affection or love.

Elizabeth is now in her mid-80s, and her early views of romance were shaped in a time when young women did not have sex outside marriage; if they did, there was punishment either from society or a contemptuous mother whose own desires had been blocked a lifetime ago.

Elizabeth will never forget one devoted couple she knew in university who dated for years. The night before graduation, they slept in the same dorm room behind a closed door; no one really knew what happened but, Elizabeth recalls, that was too much for campus norms. They were banned from the grad ceremony, handed their diplomas in private, and sent off in disgrace.

Elizabeth knows that younger women today believe the strict sexual rules of the 1950s were never really applied, that people were secretly having sex before marriage, and of course, some were. But in Elizabeth's world, most were not. She heard young men at university talk about a girl who allegedly slept around, as they described it, and she never wanted to put herself in a position to be so diminished by male judgment, however hypocritical. She quite properly earned her degree in English and psychology, attended the graduation ceremony, and got married.

The world changed, of course, in the 1960s and '70s, as women like Gloria Steinem, whom Elizabeth so admired, raised their voices calling for a female revolution. Women were able to find interesting if lower-paying jobs and eventually divorce the husbands they had married out of school, which is exactly how life unfolded for Elizabeth.

Still, the desire to follow women like Steinem and live independently, at least for those who came of age in traditional times, wasn't quite so easy to fulfill. Most felt that they had to have a man, especially a husband, to be considered a whole person.

As a single adult, Elizabeth was pretty good at blocking this feeling, but in her 50s, she decided to try the dating site Lavalife. She joined the "prime" version for people over the age of 45 and ended up in a chat group, becoming online friends with seven women and three men. They grew tight, and she is still in touch with four of them, including one of the men.

Despite the early promise of online dating, none of the women in her group met any prospects on the site. This included the men of the same age in their chat group. Two of the women, being curious, checked out the younger crowd's Lavalife and found the men from their chat group over there actively seeking dates, a discovery Elizabeth found amusing. "I think it's good for their ego," she told her friends.

Elizabeth met one of the men on a Friday night, not for a date just for an evening out. She was never sure what he was seeking and frankly believed that most people in the vast dating pool either don't know what they want or, if the opportunity arises, are spooked because they don't really want it. The guy on that one Lavalife non-date became an occasional friend to this day, mostly, she believes, because she did not flirt with him. She felt incapable of flirtation and definitely did not want to have sex with him; for Elizabeth, then and now, sex requires a near unattainable level of trust.

There is something about the desire for sex and love, as she says, that gets all tangled up because those two needs are not necessarily one and the same. After her post-divorce relationship with the charismatic abuser and the non-starter of online dating, Elizabeth decided she didn't want anyone. That part of her was finished.

And so, as she grew older, Elizabeth grew sharper, faster, at dismissing those happy little twinges of the heart. They represent vulnerability. And depending on when a woman grew up, sex might be more punitive than pleasurable. So, better to let that part of her go.

In a way, that is how society looks at older people, men and women, because much later in life, romantic yearnings are discouraged, as if they should not exist. The punishment for sexuality in the 1950s returns for old age. What do we do with this new longevity, then, if the person we become is expected to erase our humanity within?

SEXUAL HEALTH FACTS

Not to be a killjoy, but for those returning to the game, be aware of the rise in sexually transmitted diseases among older adults, some of whom are clearly getting a lot of action. According to the U.S. Centers for Disease Control and Prevention, chlamydia, gonorrhea, and syphilis more than doubled among those aged 55 plus between 2012 and 2022. In England, health data shows a strikingly similar pattern with chlamydia and gonorrhea among the most common of the age-old STIs.

CHAPTER FOURTEEN

The Lodestar

At the age of 94, Inge Fowlie misses sex with a man. She last had intercourse and what she describes as joyously rocking cunnilingus in 2020 when she was 90 and her boyfriend was 91. It all ended that year, when he died.

I write this bluntly not for shock value but to make a rather obvious point that many seemed to have missed, most recently evidenced by a conversation with a lovely woman in her late 30s, mother of two, who shouted, "*Oh my God!! You mean old people still have sex?!!!*"

Yes, they do.

For the entirety of their lives, most people want to be held in the arms of someone they care about, to be loved, emotionally and sexually, and yes, to have an orgasm which, by the way, releases dopamine, the hormone of pleasure, and oxytocin, the bonding hormone that promotes feelings of love.

Much like eating chocolate or listening to beautiful, soaring music, orgasms light up neural pathways; scientists now say that sexual climax releases blood flow in the brain, which can support healthy cognition. Who knew?

Inge makes a point of talking about sex, or her lack of it, as a normal part of life. Her last orgasm was in the late spring of 2024, she says, four months before our conversation. It was a solo endeavour, as so many are in the later years, although not for lack of yearning, the desire to find a person who is attractive, seductive, and new. Inge is an observer of humanity and an intellectual. She was raised in Germany as an orthodox Jew but in her early 20s defied the conservatism of her religion. She graduated from university and practised as a child psychologist. Inge has strong thoughts on the ways in which religions created by men destroyed the original spirituality that rose from the feminine and Mother Earth.

"We live a very short life, but history is an old story," she says. "Female goddesses go way back, but we're not told about that. It's all supposed to start with the Greeks. Well, it didn't fucking start with the Greeks."

Now she practises Buddhism. Its pragmatism, she says, is beautiful.

Inge lives in a Victorian rowhouse in downtown Toronto, its main floor renovated with wide doorways to accommodate a wheelchair, if that day ever comes. Though it hasn't yet, after turning 94, her body changed. Loyal for so long, it now seems to be betraying Inge, leaving her exhausted by midafternoon. Inexplicably, her teeth started falling out. She feels less pretty now, and Inge has always been pretty.

She keeps a schedule of meetings with the various community organizations in her life, including a group of women focused on climate change. Inge wanted to name their group Crones Protecting Our Mother Earth, but the others weren't comfortable with the C-word, so they went with WOW — Wonderful Old Women. Inge loves the power symbolized by the crone, pleased when I tell her that a young American activist named Kyrié Carpenter is reclaiming the word too.

In Inge's bedroom upstairs is a vibrator, in a Fun Factory box labelled "Your perfect moment." She is experienced in its operation and believes many older women have sex toys, and there are numerous reports that suggest she is correct. This includes a large AARP survey on sexuality that found one in three people over the age of 40 reported using a vibrator. Most were over the age of 50 and nearly one-quarter were 70 plus. Women were more likely to say they used one compared with men, at 42 percent versus 18 percent. People who identified as non-heterosexual were more likely to report using a vibrator than heterosexuals, at 66 percent and 28 percent respectively. Based on its survey of 2,506 people, AARP concluded, "As men and women get older, one thing doesn't change with time: their ability to enjoy erotic pleasure."

For Inge, using a device might fulfill her immediate sexual needs but it leaves her feeling terribly alone; she'd prefer the penis of a delightful man. What is the value of giving herself sexual pleasure when it is supposed to be an intimate, bonding experience, Inge wonders. When her orgasm ends, Inge lies still.

If there is a prevailing theme in Inge's interior life, it would be the need for touch. This yearning, she says, is like a disease that she cannot escape. Loneliness has lived alongside Inge since her husband died suddenly when she was 44 with a house full of children, and it remained, a chafing presence, even in the busy motherhood years. It was her aloneness that allowed a man she later declared a narcissist to slide into her life, as they do.

It took such precious time and energy to get rid of him that Inge remained single until her mid-80s when her daughters saw loneliness begin to devour their mother, which sounds dramatic but, as Inge says, it was true. The daughters took control, creating a dating profile on OkCupid, limiting prospective matches to men in their 80s and 90s.

At the Art Gallery of Ontario, she met the man who would become her next lover. She was wary at first but soon discovered that he was special; he loved the female body. His enthusiasm for her made Inge feel so comfortable there was never a worry about taking off her clothes, the concern that many women feel with a new partner. He was up for anything. Both older and less inhibited, they had a wilder sex life than she had decades earlier with her husband. Inge and her new boyfriend were together for three years. At 90, his erections did not always last but they existed, and as Inge says, they were fabulous.

After he died, the aloneness returned. It sits beside her over morning coffee, stalking her through the day. For a time, she was attracted to a man in her Buddhism group, imagining the spark of a new romance.

"We write to each other, and he's sick now so I have no physical relationship with him at this point, but I'm working on it, finalizing what's going to happen," Inge says in her determined way.

A few weeks later, she concluded that romance wasn't happening. "That is over," she says firmly. Still, he will be a friend, always a good thing. Older people, they need to keep trying, Inge says. Find a way to meet new partners or friends. "You might not be able to have sexual attention . . . but you need to have intimacy."

Inge talks about sexuality freely, and she wants people to understand that age has nothing to do with desire. That will never end, she says, unless people lock it away, to their detriment. As for society's refusal to countenance the idea that older people still love sex, it defies what is a natural part of life.

The truth, says Inge, is that everyone wants to be touched, not just sexually but also in an affectionate way, as in the natural embrace of children or friends.

"Older men need it too. They love it!" she says. "Everything alive needs to be touched until death do us part."

Inge has had a long life, and as she contemplates women in their 40s or 50s who are statistically likely to reach her age, it makes sense to her, that society will change its views on mature sexuality, if only because there will be more older women who don't accept antiquated ways. "Hopefully we will be able to write our own story."

For Inge, that story goes back to the beginning of time, history as she knows it, when goddesses ruled. Now, this unprecedented longevity is finally reigniting the phase of life she loves: the crone, in all her power, rising.

• • •

As a feminist and anthropologist who leads a company focused on cultural marketing, Johanna Faigelman is wise to the patterns of history. She does not speak of ancient religious patriarchs' elimination of female leaders but knows that we are entering another dangerous time, when rapid change fuels fear.

When a society dominated by men feels a collective loss of control, there is often a backlash against women or those considered vulnerable, such as immigrants or members of 2SLGBTQI+ communities. Women's bodies, Faigelman says, are more easily governed than the revolution brought to us by the societal upturning expected from artificial intelligence.

In such comparisons, complexities abound, and there is much going on, politically, economically, and digitally, to create unease. Still, Faigelman sees parallels between today's harsh politics and the Victorian era when the rapid pace of change created by the industrial revolution seemed unfathomable. How better to control the uncontrollable than by dictating the societal values of women? Women had to become exceedingly pious. Subservient. And women of a certain class had to spend their days in the drawing room playing the pianoforte or embroidering in a corner chair usually near a window, where one might peer outside, longingly, but only on the down low.

Those who rebelled risked the hysteria diagnosis, Faigelman says, and the male medical establishment decreed that the cure for this disorder was the removal of the uterus, a brutal medical procedure. That misogyny is rooted in the word *hysterectomy*, she notes, the commonly used term for the same operation in modern times, although for much different reasons.

Today, as technological transformation threatens our livelihoods, Faigelman sees an intense anger among some men who feel disenfranchised, believing they matter less. Social media has amplified a flourishing movement against diversity, equity, and inclusion policies in the workplace; as discussed in Chapter Ten, the backlash also extends to medical research.

"The level of anger against women has never been higher than this moment in time," Faigelman says. "As an anthropologist what I've observed is that there are periods of time in history when you have that anger, and it usually refers to there being a cultural tension happening in society. You have a rising level of anger and a rising level of power colliding with each other, because you get angrier and angrier when you feel you are losing. You're not angry when you're winning."

If the very real threat from artificial intelligence is not sufficiently profound, Faigelman says we are also entering an economic and cultural shift. Thanks to the extended female lifespan, tens of millions of older women in North America will wield immense purchasing power, although it may take men awhile to notice.

This does not mean that older women all follow the same politics. Clearly they do not. But it is a revolution of demographics, the rise of older women who, if it needs stating, are of an age when they care less what others think. As the coffee mugs say, "No fucks left to give."

Considering the so-called invisibility of women, we shall see if those who seek to control what cannot be contained will recognize this incoming female power. After decades of gender battles, the losses and draws, longevity just might give women the ultimate win.

• • •

Instead of immediately launching into a conversation about a 2.0 version of the 1960s sexual revolution, here is a question: Why do we refuse to acknowledge sexuality among much older women?

I put this to Laura Tamblyn Watts, an advocate for older adults, in a conversation that began after I interviewed her for my *Toronto Star* podcast, *How to Live to 100 or Die Trying*. Our chat continued, with enthusiasm, in the elevator ride and into the atrium of the Well building in downtown Toronto where the *Star* makes its home; we (politely) interrupted each other until agreeing to follow up in an official interview so as not to let these ideas go to waste. Tamblyn Watts was at her home, overlooking the Bay of Fundy in Nova Scotia, when we connected by phone for the second round.

Right now, readers, I am mostly giving Tamblyn Watts the floor. She will hold it for a while, until we all take a beat below.

The inability to accept sexuality among older women begins with the statistical shift toward living to 100, a lifespan expectation that most of us still cannot comprehend.

"We have a hard time grasping longevity," she says. "I was reading something that talked about why we have mid-life crises, and the thesis is that it's not a mid-life crisis: It's a second-life crisis because we get to our 40s and 50s and that should mean, on an evolutionary basis, that we die. Until about 100 years ago, on average, that was the case. So, we actually don't know what to do with ourselves.

"We don't want to think about women who are not reproductive having sex because if we think about what the purpose of sex is and the sort of patriarchal notion, it's to have kids. So, after you've had kids, you kind of should be done. We just haven't grappled with the idea of women's sexuality that is not in service, somehow, to men.

"We also think about women in relational terms: my aunt, my mother, my grandmother. As we block people into those relational roles, it adds a degree of uncomfortable familiarity where sexuality and sexual intimacy mostly do not play a role. (Nobody wants to acknowledge that Grandma is out in the world flirting, let alone enjoying a rush of post-coital oxytocin.)

"All of these things are fusing together and then add on top of it this clear, clear sense of ageism . . . the sort of deterioration of female beauty which is valorized in that maiden period and maintained to a certain degree for the mother period and then it kind of drops right off. Then we get these notions of purposelessness, so we don't know what the role of older women is in society, and all of that comes to a morass."

Let's stop here.

It is true: Women have been impacted by biology at almost every life stage, and the male gaze, with its inherent demands, starts early and ends early, which is often a relief. As Inge Fowlie would say, this is the outcome of the religious patriarchy that rid the world of the original feminine power, only to view women as playthings or child-bearing vessels.

Change, of course, is ever thus. When driven by demographics, it is inevitable and sometimes cultural shifts require a few brave women to set ideas free. In this context, we are talking about menopause and the growing number of celebrities, such as Halle Berry, Salma Hayek, Shania Twain, Gwyneth Paltrow, and Angelina Jolie, who have discussed their experience and are anything but the old trope used to depict post-menopausal women.

"There's no expiration dates for women," Salma Hayek has said. "That has to go. Because you can kick ass at any age. You can hold your own at any age, you can dream at any age, you can be romantic at age [*sic*].

"We have the right to be loved for who we are at the place that we are. We're not just here to make babies, we're not just here to baby the man. We're not just here to service everything and everyone around us and then when the kids go away . . . it's almost like expiration date for you as a woman. It's a misunderstanding that has been going around for centuries."

Menopause and perimenopause are having a moment, in no small part due to the collective voice of the Gen Xers and millennials who are demanding a better understanding and treatment of symptoms. Using the power of social media, they expect more from a society that previously mocked, ignored, or just didn't know what to do with this natural female experience.

It is also worth listening to much older women about other life transformations.

Kate Chung believes the long-ago hippies and their free-love movement mostly benefitted men, though birth control pills saved many women from unwanted pregnancies. Now in her 80s, Chung was married at that time so did not partake, but her perspective shows that revolutions are best evaluated through the eyes of the beholder.

Chung's time is now devoted to advocacy for accessibility in housing design so people with disabilities can remain at home and avoid institutions. And while the sex lives of older women are not part of her discussion repertoire, Chung has worthy insight on thoughtful decisions that might get one to a 2.0 version for older women's sexuality.

Divorced decades ago, she raised three children on her own and for a long time struggled to pay for rent and food. Romance wasn't exactly top of mind, but in her 50s, fearing that her judgment was skewed after a few failed relationships, Chung decided to engage in "practice dating." She bought a companion ad in the *Toronto Star*'s classified section and described herself as a "joyous feminist and activist" to weed out the unsuitables.

Practice dating quickly offered an important lesson: Listen to your intuition.

So many of us want to believe a person's lofty romantic claims (otherwise known as love bombing) that we ignore our instincts, our innate ability to read the tiniest of warnings. And since there are good people out there, our intuition can also show us when someone's presence makes us feel calm and safe.

Kate met Doug. She liked him, quite a lot. But there was a problem. Her brain insisted she not rush into a relationship too soon. Her intuition told her to keep this lovely man.

She listened to the latter. They've been together for 30 years.

"I realized that I always had judgment — I just hadn't used it!" Kate says.

Now, when she is joined by fellow Raging Grannies at the edge of the Scarborough Bluffs singing self-composed ditties about nursing homes as jails, about their preference to throw themselves off the cliff rather than die in an institution, Doug is at her side, taking photographs.

In my research for this book, many women turned our conversations toward their desire for companionship and, quite naturally, their longing for sexual intimacy. Years after her partner died, Pat Dunn still loved Dave and missed the richness of their life together; that doesn't mean her desire for intimacy ended in his absence. "I still get horny," she says, laughing. And yet Pat will no longer risk rejection, feeling pushed aside because of her age, her wrinkles (however attractive), and her lack of money. Who would open their heart and step into a world knowing some suitors, with their own bodily vicissitudes, feel they are in a position to judge?

Let's also acknowledge the men who experience challenges. In addition to erectile dysfunction, some of which can be alleviated with medication, many older men are lost to solitude after a partner dies. Some want a new companion, but others, well, their behaviour doesn't inspire much success on the older adult dating scene.

I once met with a group of 80-something men, researching male isolation for a *Toronto Star* podcast episode that was part of a fellowship with the Gerontological Society of America. As a journalist, I love anecdotes that are counterintuitive or perplexing. And one after another, these men spoke about their attempts to get out of the house and join social clubs, only to discover the membership was dominated by women of their vintage. There was too much female energy, they said, too much talking. It was so overwhelming that some men claimed they left, never to return. Most were widowers. They preferred to remain at home.

When I asked if they might not enjoy the attention of so many women, the men looked at me as if I had just arrived from a galaxy far away. Older men don't easily express their feelings, so I do not know if this was related to a generational disinclination toward female friendship or a simple desire to hang out with guys, but it does not bode well for octogenarian dating, especially with a dwindling pool of potential male suitors.

The challenge of navigating new relationships is even harder for those who do not come from a comparatively powerful position in society.

Where do older queer women go to meet other women? As it gets harder, finding a friendly space just to be yourself is increasingly important. In Colorado, some women drive 90 minutes to attend a Monday morning conversation group in an 2SLGBTQI+ community centre. Dr. Carey Candrian facilitates these meetings of older queer women. As the director of LGBTQ+ research and community engagement at the University of Colorado School of Medicine, Dr. Candrian first arrived at the centre as a speaker. She soon discovered that a fledgling women's conversation group was about to lose its space to a program for men.

"I knew it couldn't," Dr. Candrian says. "It's so hard to find community in general, and especially for these older adults. We started with four people. The centre said, 'If you can't get the numbers higher, we will take this group down.' So, I started bringing friends as guest speakers on physical therapy and health and everything in between, and we now have a stable group of 15. It's remarkable. It's really just a place to talk and have fun. It's not a therapy group. It's not a dating group. It's just a place to be in community with each other."

This companionship matters deeply to the women whose partners have died, she says. One woman in her 80s arrives every Monday morning, grateful she has the freedom to be herself.

After living openly for much of her life, she moved into an assisted-living residence six years earlier, and initial chats with fellow residents always led to the same questions: "Were you married?" and "Do you have children?" When she said no, her neighbours stopped engaging.

In a time when many older adults are moving into retirement homes, the privately operated residences that promise three meals a day and daily activities, some women quickly realize that hiding their sexuality is the only way to avoid social ostracization.

"It's still a huge deal," Dr. Candrian says. "You have to lead these closeted lives and are never able to talk about your past or have the opportunity to really have an intimate relationship as you age."

During our conversation, I tell Dr. Candrian about my discussion with Laura Tamblyn Watts, on the potential that longevity, and fewer men, might offer some women the opportunity to explore a sexual fluidity that they had to hide earlier in life. Dr. Candrian wonders if some women would have the strength to explore new relationships after following traditional values for so long. And yet others might be inspired, she says, by the freedom to find love of their choosing.

• • •

Men have long benefitted from the power and privilege needed to build a life resilient to age.

This is particularly evident, says Tamblyn Watts, in the attentiveness of pharmaceutical companies to erectile dysfunction, which understandably can be a blow to self-esteem. For years now, 80-year-old men have apparently been able to perform with a teenaged vigour, since Viagra stays in the body for several hours while Cialis remains for 36. (It's not the erection that lasts this long, just the ability to get one). This has helped many men remain impervious to this facet of aging, but times are changing.

"Now, in so many ways, it is the women's turn," Tamblyn Watts says. And it has nothing to do with taking a pill. Instead, she believes that a female focus on well-being, including hormone replacement, can extend middle age to last through the 60s and into the 70s.

"And the notions of fitness and health — and for that matter, a little nip and tuck — also push back against the idea that a number [age] equals something ugly. Now, it doesn't," she says.

"This is a new part of the women's movement. It's only just had this opportunity to blossom because of the conversations around things like women's autonomy, choices around health care, the ability to have different relationships around children, whether it be not having children or IVF or having children in later life. It's really the first generations where this has been possible," she says. "I think the world is going to be surprised to see a whole new sexual revolution coming, which is going to be driven by older women."

Our original discussion started when I asked her thoughts on the choices available to heterosexual women who outlive men. Tamblyn Watts suggests some may embrace an à la carte selection of relationships to fulfill their needs. The options are plentiful from friendship to practical polyamory and much, much more. But, she says, the advantages of sexual sharing are not entirely clear.

"Is this helpful to women or is it another sort of misogynistic, patriarchal use and misuse of women? I don't know," she says. "Will they find it liberating because they go to an over-60 Tinder style hookup or Grindr kind of app where everyone understands the rules, and is that going to be empowering, an opportunity to hook up and explore that kind of sexual encounter? Or is that the only thing that's available to leverage into meaningful, interpersonal relations? I don't know. But we've never had choices like this before."

Welcome to revelations of longevity. What it all comes down to, with these ideas, these concepts, is the desire to live with vitality, yes, and to share it with people who care about each other. It's hard to look upon an additional 40 or so years of life with anticipation if it will be spent craving connections that do not exist. And while there is something to be said for carefree fun, it's not clear how sustaining quick encounters could be when all we've got is time.

As Inge Fowlie says, everyone needs intimacy, and intimacy is not just the physical. She also says older people need to work to find each other. Maybe the best way to manage the unknown is to take the advice of Kate Chung and follow our intuition, the truth-telling north star that guides us forward. Now that's a connection for life.

CHAPTER FIFTEEN

Pat

In the days before Pat's Facebook epiphany, on the temporary comfort of her sister's couch, she started writing in her notebook, just like she did before meeting Dave. This time, instead of her conditions for a new man, she focused on housing and the ways it might help not just with shelter but with her entire well-being.

The grief she felt when her five-year-old son died was indescribable, but she shared it with her husband, daughter, and friends. Her daughter lives in another country now, and Pat's friends, all retired, have scattered across the country, as people do. The loss of Dave left her adrift, with an emptiness that felt like poison lodged under her skin. It was inescapable.

Knowing she could not stay in her sister's apartment much longer, Pat researched loneliness and discovered she was on track for a perilous decline. So in 2019, at the age of 68, Pat took stock of her life.

Pat liked to work through problems with pen and paper. It organized her mind. Writing in tiny letters to preserve space, she started with the obvious — how to make money. Pat has partial hearing loss, which made working difficult, and after applying for online jobs, she concluded that most were scams. Her options were limited.

Next came housing. Yes, she was on a 10-year wait-list for a rent-geared-to-income apartment in Peterborough, after weeping in the parking lot, but she couldn't sleep in her sister's living room for the next decade, nor would her sister live that long.

Pat made a checklist of traditional housing options that she had already pursued. Rooming houses. Hard no. Buying a condo. Impossible. Renting an apartment. Unaffordable. The short-term winter rentals needed when the trailer park closed for the season were too expensive. It all came down to money, and when she reconciled the cost of living in Canada with her retirement income, including a workplace pension that paid roughly $700 per month, a moment of clarity arrived. She had two years before her savings were gone.

Pat, a woman with a bachelor of science degree in nursing from McMaster University who once ran programs in a large public health department, was sliding into homelessness. Pat grew angry. "This is just wrong!" she said to her sister. "Canada shouldn't be shutting out people living on low pensions but not in poverty."

She didn't want subsidized housing, not if she could find another way. Nor did she want to live in a rundown apartment building, walking past a long row of closed doors until she'd lock herself inside her own unit. Pat envisioned a house with a small backyard and people with whom she would share the space, not every moment but the occasional home-cooked meal or intelligent conversation.

It was true, Pat realized, that she had high standards. She wanted to be around women who were interesting and interested.

Superior education was not a requirement, but intelligence, yes. The public health planner in Pat wanted to create a community of women who were curious, well-read, who could talk about something other than topics that ended with a flat "oh really," like recipes or grandchildren, although those were also fine with limits.

Pat wrote it all out in long hand. Closing the notebook, she logged on to Facebook and created that post, detailing the problem and posing the question "Am I the only woman in this predicament?"

As the weeks passed and she read the responses to her post, all with personal stories, it occurred to Pat that this was more than a search for roommates. She realized the arc of her life — marriage, a big house, the yacht club membership, divorce, Dave's death, and her financial comedown — was not so rare. Some women had struggled all along; others had graduated from university, raised children, divorced or buried husbands, found interesting jobs, and in their later years could no longer afford to live.

Pat connected with a woman from Peterborough who seemed compatible, as much as you can tell through online chatting. In April, when the trailer park opened, Pat flew back to Ontario. She met the woman. They liked each other. They decided to find a place to rent and soon found a third woman to share the cost.

Pat sold her trailer that summer, paid off her debts, and moved into a rundown motel that is best described as seedy. At least it was affordable. At the time, the local vacancy rates for houses were so low there was nothing available, nothing affordable, but Pat had been speaking online with a landlord, a woman who owned several properties and was rather miraculously considering the purchase of a house that she would rent to them.

As all this unfolded in the summer of 2019, Pat, the planner, and three other women launched the non-profit group Senior

Women Living Together. At first it was a collection of women on Facebook, over time, SWLT grew to 2,500 members in Ontario. With Pat at the helm, SWLT added a volunteer board of directors of members and women with experience in corporate leadership. It now has a website, a platform for women aged 55 and older "where you can learn about shared living, find compatible home mates, and together find suitable rental accommodation."

As Pat jokes, it's like making a match in dating. She doesn't get involved in the matchmaking, the individual women sort out whether they can live together. Who does the housework? Can you be trusted not to eat the last of my lasagna? How can an introvert extricate themself from an extrovert without offending?

In the beginning, Pat spent her days talking. To potential landlords, selling them on the idea of renting to quiet older women, which seemed like a no-brainer. She also connected with women who were desperate for someone who understood.

At her tiny desk in the home she shared with two roommates, Pat's days stretched into evening, sometimes spending 14 hours or more working on SWLT as the chief organizer, therapist, and dreamer, hoping to help women in other provinces launch chapters of their own.

Sharing the rent three ways has helped Pat save a bit of money each month; that makes her feel accomplished and a bit giddy. In demand for her insights on housing, Pat drives her old car to give speeches; this replacement for the Corolla is also etched in rust.

Sometimes she feels hopeful. Women across the country are reaching out for advice, with plans to create their own version of Senior Women Living Together. Ever the project manager, Pat shares her best practices, if they get that far. Mostly she listens as politicians make promises on housing; none of them speak about real affordability for women like her.

It all seems so long ago now, that epiphany on her sister's couch when Pat realized that financial stress and aloneness were not solely her fate but reality for a much wider population. It was a public health crisis, a contagion with no easy cure.

HOUSING FACTS

In its third annual national housing survey, Habitat for Humanity Canada examined the impact of unaffordability on mental health along with a growing economic and generational divide.

- Fifty-eight percent of survey respondents believe that a middle class still exists, but 82 percent are worried that the lack of affordable housing is contributing to shrinking the middle class.
- Nearly 60 percent of Canadians worry about sacrificing basic needs like food, clothing, and education to afford their rent or mortgage payments.
- Two-thirds of Gen Z Canadians and almost half of millennials have considered delaying having children because they cannot afford suitable housing.

CHAPTER SIXTEEN

Home

At the older women's housing co-op, a stately six-bedroom home in Winnipeg's Riverview neighbourhood, Beverly Suek has a policy for almost any issue conceivable, all in pursuit of equanimity in co-living.

In her early 80s, with a long and busy professional career focused on proper governance and organizational oversight, Beverly appreciates a good set of rules. The women's co-op has a basic policy for illness in communal spaces, from colds to COVID, including the disposal of used tissues. Guidelines focus on food, shared tasks, and conflict resolution. But the pièce de resistance, in a home of six single women, is what Beverly calls the policy on men.

Technically, it is the policy on romance. According to the official document written by Beverly, the co-op founder and Order of Manitoba recipient for decades of community activism, it is designed to place thoughtful limits on the visitations of men, women, and non-binary individuals.

Special friends can stay a night or three but not too long. "Please let your floor partner know in case they encounter a stranger," the policy states. "We want to make sure roommates feel comfortable in the house and can wander in pyjamas if they want."

Ideally, the women agree in advance on a secret signal to their roommates, an alert, if you will, that a romantic encounter is unfolding. There is a different rule for "spontaneous absences." If a woman decides to seize the moment and enjoy a night elsewhere, she's asked to text her housemates. "It's just that we might wonder if you're okay if you don't come home," the policy paper states.

You might have figured out that the co-op rules are intended not just for good order but to create a home that is full of life, much as it was when Beverly raised a blended family of seven children here, all coming and going, before she and her husband turned it into a bed and breakfast.

It is a two-storey brown brick house with round white pillars and an upper-level porch overlooking the park across the street. After her husband died, one of her sons lived here with his family; in 2014, when he was ready to move on, Beverly bought the home back from him.

Having decided that she no longer wanted to live alone, Beverly created the Women's Housing Initiative Manitoba. She built a sunroom, a new kitchen, and set up the co-op organizational structure, eventually selling a $30,000 share to each woman accepted. Communal living, Beverly believes, offers older women affordable housing and releases them from the dread of loneliness and social isolation. She designed the kitchen with conviviality in mind, adding space at the island for at least four barstools so some can chat while others chop and stir.

The first woman to move in was a United Church minister. She had been living in a furnished apartment after separating from her husband.

"I was going to say it was love at first sight, but not," says Beverly, laughing. "We liked each other, and she has been here ever since. The only thing she brought with her was a garlic press, and if she ever leaves, she has to get her garlic press back."

The minister rented the biggest bedroom, and she pays roughly $1,000 a month. Others slowly arrived and took smaller rooms, most paying about $700. With the $30,000 downpayment from each and the monthly fees that cover expenses, housekeeping, lawn cutting, and snow removal, this shared existence seems to be clicking. There is, to be sure, a legal agreement that requires the return of that $30,000 if a person departs, but not before a replacement lives in the home for a 12-month trial period during which the newcomer and the existing inhabitants decide if they can co-exist.

Co-living, or at least the idea of it, is part of a growing conversation about how and where we will live in our later years. Mostly found through word-of-mouth, it is worthy of consideration, especially with a good legal agreement. There are a lot of issues that can crop up over the years. Dementia is one of them. What happens when an individual can no longer care for herself? Some legal agreements anticipate such future issues, which define protections for all.

A temporary version of co-living is offered by Canada HomeShare; it pairs younger people, often students seeking affordable rent, with an older adult who has an empty room or two at home. And thanks to advance planning, its staff can help navigate any friction caused by dirty dishes in the sink or generational misunderstandings. Equanimity is the goal.

Mind you, it's not for everyone. When contemplating a co-ownership commitment, investing equity into a shared house, it's best to remember that people can be quirky. However unlikely, breakout factions within a home can lead to a tense morning coffee. The benefits of shared living can eliminate isolation and financial stress quite beautifully, but pitfalls do exist.

While the idea of older women sharing a home is not new, at least in a casual sense, interest is growing, and with good reason since more than one million Canadian women aged 65 and older lived alone in 2021. While many can support themselves, many others cannot.

This demographic shift is inspiring new housing ideas, and if there is one truism I've learned, women are resourceful. Innovation comes from many sources. The desire to fill a home with the energy of other humans led to Beverly Suek's co-housing in Winnipeg. Desperation launched Pat Dunn's search for roommates, and purpose led to her non-profit, Senior Women Living Together. The so-called Golden Girls of Port Perry, Ontario, calculated the longevity of their savings and decided to pool resources on a beautiful home within walking distance of downtown.

In apartments or condos from Vancouver to Hamilton, older residents are creating social supports for neighbours, all of whom want to age in place. Colloquially called NORCs, for naturally occurring retirement communities, these mostly high-rise buildings have a significant percentage of residents who are aging and offer the pragmatism of population density. With so many older people in one location, governments could fund programs to help aging in place, instead of people's current trajectory to expensive hospitals and nursing homes.

I've written extensively on the value of NORC programs that originated in New York City housing co-ops. Their early success led to state and city funding for programs in buildings, with staff to organize fitness programs, do nutrition checks, schedule medical appointments, and generally ensure the well-being of the people who live there.

Canada needs housing that doesn't crush the most vulnerable, and while the official list of those in need includes Indigenous people, Black people, and single mothers, low-income older women (and men) are always right up there. And yet the problem with housing never ends.

So it was illuminating when Tim Richter, considered the country's top housing expert, said Canada's official housing data is "blind to the needs" of many, including older women living in unaffordability best described as severe.

Many women with a fixed (and low) retirement income spend 80 percent — or more — on rent and food, leaving them incredibly vulnerable to even minute price increases, says Richter who, among his many roles, is president and CEO of the Canadian Alliance to End Homelessness. "So what does she do? Goes to the food bank. Tries to live with family, and if she doesn't have family, she scrimps and saves and makes ends meet while her health deteriorates."

Something has to be done. In 2023, Scotiabank economist Rebekah Young called on Canada to double its social housing stock saying, "The moral case to urgently build out Canada's anemic stock of social housing has never been stronger. The economic case is equally compelling."

Announced in 2017, Canada's National Housing Strategy was widely criticized for its lack of success in building homes that were affordable for those on a low income. Much was promised, with little achieved. Now in 2025, we have a new prime minister with a new plan.

Roughly five months after his April 28 election, Prime Minister Mark Carney's office announced a $13 billion fund to build "deeply affordable and community housing for low-income households, and partner with private market developers to build affordable homes for the Canadian middle class."

A new housing agency called Build Canada Homes, the government said, will use modular housing, a "faster, cheaper alternative" to traditional construction while building on federal land. The agency will have access to the government's federally-owned land portfolio. It will offer financing "incentives" and "leverage public lands for housing so projects are derisked and private builders can focus on building."

Some are greeting it with cautious optimism. As housing expert Tim Richter wrote for the Canadian Alliance to End Homelessness, if properly executed, it could be a major breakthrough, with a particular focus on easing homelessness. For Carney's plan to succeed, many disparate actions need to align, Richter wrote, including a new definition of affordability and a focus on housing for those who need it immediately.

For now, Richter warned, Carney's plan "risks trying to be everything, everywhere, all at once."

• • •

Even if this new plan succeeds, it won't change the fact that after decades of neglect, Canada has a lot of catching up to do. It wasn't always this way.

Nearly 100 years ago, housing captured the attention of the federal government. In the 1930s, Canada passed legislation meant to increase its overall housing stock, promote private market growth, and support the construction of low-rent homes. (Sounds familiar.) As the Second World War ended and soldiers arrived home, Ottawa created a Crown corporation to oversee a wartime housing program; over the next eight years, it built 45,930 units.

A wholehearted investment in social housing began in the mid-1960s with federal legislation offering loan transfers to the provinces for construction of public housing that the provinces would own. The same law gave housing loans to municipalities and private non-profit corporations. For the next 20 years, federal money transfers helped provinces build, operate, and subsidize rent in social housing units, including non-profit co-operatives.

As the 1980s progressed, Canada slowly started cutting its housing investment, and by 1992, it ended the federal co-operative housing program. Ottawa's enthusiasm for such investments came to an end in the late 1990s, when it downloaded housing to provinces, ending a program that built nearly 60,000 homes for low- and moderate-income Canadians.

Some federal investment returned in the early 2000s, but its impact was dismissed as marginal. With a void to fill, rental stock in cities shifted to investor-owned condos. This is not affordable housing. Even with slight rent declines, and a decidedly struggling condo market, the average cost of a one-bedroom Vancouver apartment in December 2024 was $2,500. In Toronto, it was $2,360.

Condo investors played a role in the financialization of housing in large Canadian cities; in some European cities, the privatization of public assets is driven by private real estate companies. Canada's social housing is facing the same risk.

When public housing was downloaded in the 1990s, many municipalities agreed to operate and subsidize the buildings, and those arrangements are reaching their expiration dates. As Tim Richter says, it makes them prime fodder for hedge-fund operators who, it is feared, might get a deal on old buildings, pay for upgrades, and then rent them at market value, further diminishing Canada's already low stock of subsidized housing.

"Older adults, especially those on fixed incomes, are especially vulnerable during the housing crisis because there's very little housing stock for them to live in, and what's available will continuously increase in cost in a way that they can't absorb, they can't cope with," Richter said. "This is going to be a bigger and bigger issue as Canada's population ages."

Where does all this leave women who look to the future? One version predicts misery, stretching across these extra decades that, after an internal cost-benefit analysis, some no longer want.

Others try to fill the void. In Montreal, a woman teaches classes on how to co-exist in a rented house with strangers. Others advise on ways to empty our cupboards, literally, and create an efficient life. What do we fight to hold on to, and how might it feel if we let go? It is an evolution of thinking.

Erin Harris tells women to start planning for their future by the age of 55.

Now in her early 80s, Harris is called the Queen by her friends. She is a feminist activist and a coordinator with the Older Women's Network, an advocacy group that operates co-op housing on the Esplanade in Toronto, in the same building as a co-op for older artists.

Before her divorce at the age of 39, Harris lived in a nice single-family house with a husband she supported, she says, while he earned an MBA. Later, advocacy work exposed her to the struggles of single women, and Harris realized she'd be wise to prepare for her own financial survival, with a focus on affordable housing. Now she tells other women to do the same.

We spend the early half of our adult lives accumulating possessions, she says, constantly striving to attain more, and if circumstances one day require upheaval, most of us are so weighed down by our things, we cannot see a way forward.

Harris also believes every woman, particularly those who are single, should contemplate the health changes that can come with age and decide, financially, if her living arrangements can help manage whatever fate arrives. She asks women, What if you get cancer? Or a stroke? How will you financially survive if you are alone? Free your money, and yourself, Harris says, by changing your perspective toward those possessions, be they houses, furniture, or six sets of English bone china.

During her evolutionary period, Harris helped friends furnish their cottages with her old sofas and donated furniture to charities. With every departure, she felt lighter.

The next step, she says, requires curiosity. Once you can envision a life with fewer possessions, and it's a process, start scoping out affordable ways to live. In some cities, the options are not plentiful, so it might mean a step down, but, she says, less financial outflow means more inner peace.

A few decades before necessary put your name on a wait-list for affordable housing or co-ops, if those co-ops are still adding new names, she says. Live simply. Be nimble, especially if you have an inkling that longevity is in your bones.

These conversations about affordable NORCs or a Golden Girls co-ownership approach all spark interest in opportunities scattered across Canada.

To digress for a moment, the Golden Girls' shared housing would not have existed without the advocacy of older women such as Martha Casson who fought the local council's refusal to issue building permits to a home that would be shared by older adults. A forward-thinking builder's first attempt to get permits was denied because council claimed it would become a retirement home. His plans were denied again a few years later, due to the unfathomable idea that women in their 60s would buy a house and live together. This time, Casson took the cause of age discrimination to the Ontario Human Rights Commission, which told council to smarten up.

The win for older women made headlines and caught the attention of a local member of provincial parliament who introduced legislation named for the Golden Girls, and while it did not pass second reading, the concept of shared housing is now included in Ontario's Planning Act.

The work of Casson and others speaks to the power of older women who turn their attention to advocacy. This bodes well for the future, but every step forward shouldn't require a fight.

Among NORC programs, the timing is serendipitous. Their popularity is soaring, and it is usually women who launch the weekly coffee chats or yoga sessions in their buildings. Once established, the programs multiply. It is time governments recognized the health benefits of NORC programs and provided legitimate support instead of relying on the free labour of older women.

For shared rentals, at least with Montreal's Radical Resthomes, challenges persist.

Janet Torge is the founder of Radical Resthomes. She has tried for more than a decade to find the right mix of personalities to rent a quintessential Montreal home, a stately old house with five, six, or seven bedrooms that, as Janet says, was built in a time when Catholic French-Canadian families had a lot of children. Declining birth rates changed housing demands, creating a new opportunity for shared living among older renters who, at least from a landlord's perspective, are less likely to host beer pong parties than students. Renting a $1,000-per-month room in a beautiful Montreal home seems worth the effort.

Torge is certainly trying. In 2024, when she was 77 years old, she was in her 13th year with Radical Resthomes, holding home-share training sessions for prospective roommates. It's a tricky business, finding the right personality matches, assuaging fears, and helping extricate others from their current housing and into a shared rental, all at the same time.

She's not doing this because of her relentless altruism.

"Sometimes I just want to throw up my hands and say 'No, I just I can't do it anymore.' But *I* need the solution," Torge says. "So, I just keep going because I'm one of the women that you're talking about who has worked forever and I'm running out of money. I have no pension. I have no savings. I just live on a prayer."

She has lived a life of productivity. In the early 1970s, Torge and two other women created the Vancouver Rape Relief Society, described as the first rape crisis centre in Canada. Later, in Montreal, she distributed educational handbooks about birth control or babies for the Montreal Health Press; she worked as a prenatal teacher and a doula. She has produced documentary films and, throughout all of this, was a freelance journalist.

"I'm just all over the place, and that is how I have kept my head above water. And it is true. Once I learn a job, I get bored and can't figure out why I'm still there," she says, laughing. "But doing that when you're in your 30s, 40s, and 50s is very different than doing that when you're 77 years old. If I compete for work against 50-year-olds, I lose for no other reason than because 50-year-olds have quite a good job history as well. I have more job history, but it's not, for instance, in the area that means that I'm better than they are. I'm looking at this thinking, Do I have to move in with my son? I mean, Is this what it's going to come down to?"

When we spoke, Torge lived alone in an apartment in Montreal's Mile End, spending most of her payments from CPP and OAS on rent, with next to nothing left after groceries. Until now, she has always lived with others, in a commune or with friends, and later in a duplex with her son and his wife; when their marital situation changed, she moved out to keep the parents of her grandchild under the same roof. This is what mothers do.

Now, Radical Resthomes is her best option, if only she could find the right mix of people. Shared living requires a certain philosophy that is amenable to the occasional intransigence and peccadilloes of others. One couple was quite interested, but their conservatism would not have blended with a couple who ascribed to a more bohemian lifestyle. One individual might be a vegan and unable to exist in a kitchen with meat. The reality is that many of us become increasingly affixed to our beliefs and life choices as we age; shared living requires a serendipity of spirit.

With no successful shared housing in place, at least not in 2024, Torge organizes workshops, calling people together to discuss shelter in a time of aging. She invites 12 people in person, most of whom range in age from their 60s to mid-70s. They discuss life, finances, pensions, children, and downsizing. A few are couples. There are no single men, although they are, she says, most welcome. The majority are single women with little money and, Torge says, a fear of ending up impoverished in a nursing home.

"What I'm trying to do now is find the first group to live in a house, five or six people. Tons of people love the idea of shared housing but it's for seniors, and the trouble is with people my age, and I'm 77, the idea of downsizing and moving is like 'I can't do it.'"

Her next plan, naturally, involves a downsizing workshop, and if all goes as planned, she will organize a small group of hopefully like-minded people who will spend a year purging old possessions with emotional support from Radical Resthomes.

It is, Torge believes, an idea of prescient value for boomers and, at least in Montreal, for landlords trying to rent those old family mansions that, she says, are losing their purchasing appeal with young smaller families.

It is an unexpected outcome of ever-changing demographics. The national trend toward declining birth rates also means fewer children to care for us in our old age, which is all the more reason to find a roommate who will notice if you don't make it down for dinner.

FEMINISM FACTS

Among millennials and Generation X, near equal numbers of women and men identify as feminists, according to the Survey Center on American Life. For millennials, that translates to 52 percent of men and 54 percent of women. In the Gen X generation, the male to female comparison is 43 percent compared to 49 percent.

Men's support for women's equality lessens among the older and younger generations. Only 38 percent of boomer men identify as feminists compared to 50 percent of boomer women. The gender divide widens dramatically among the youngest adults, Gen Z, where 61 percent of women support the label compared to 43 percent of men.

CHAPTER SEVENTEEN

Onward

A few years ago, a young British singer-songwriter named Paris Paloma released a song called "Labour." Paloma channels the voice of a woman who bought into the fairytale of a relationship; realizing the physical and emotional work her man required, she is exhausted. And angry.

For many reasons, the lyrics are compelling. Let's start with the fact that Paloma was born in 1999, which makes her part of Generation Z. Lately, there has been much discussion about Gen Z, claiming that its early idealism, the reimagining of, say, gender roles, has been discarded. We are told Gen Zs are the new boomers, seeking the convention of marriage and a house in the suburbs, with tradwife appeal.

But along came Paloma's song. A year after its 2023 release, "Labour" had more than 308 million streams on Spotify and 57 million views on YouTube, not to mention millions of inspired conversations after going viral on TikTok.

Maybe it is a wary recognition of the (boomer) life that Gen Z allegedly bought into, but a YouTube compilation of Paloma's live performances shows thousands of young women singing — often shouting — every word in this lyrically intense song. That is emotional commitment. As one commenter said, "This isn't just a song, it's an ANTHEM!"

These are early days, but the buzz around "Labour" is that it has launched a viral feminist movement for a new generation. Where the 1960s revolution enabled women to get out of the house and work — with the life-altering benefit of birth control — this viral version addresses a different point. First-wave feminists may have won their independence, but to have it all, they had to do it all. Work. Run the household. Do laundry. Take the lead in child-rearing. And look after the emotional, physical, sexual, and sometimes fantastical notions of their husbands.

Paloma's song (understandably) does not mention the future economic impact of this female labour — the motherhood penalty and the gender pension gap. But the recognition of inequity by so many young women creates the opportunity for a profound conversation on the gender pension gap. This is how change begins, at the start of a career when knowledge gives women the power to choose a helpful partner and seek a job with the best possible salary, benefits, and pension.

It is an eternal truth that the person we choose as a spouse will impact our success in life and retirement.

As feminist economist Dr. Tammy Schirle says, an equitable partnership would consider the woman's future loss of income and pension due to maternity leave, and if that marriage leads to divorce, the monetary sacrifice of single parenting, which the woman typically handles. There is great value in educating young women — and men — about equality in marriage.

The fact that Gen Z women are so captivated that the song has hundreds of millions of downloads, not to mention real-time conversations, should inspire banks, insurers, or governments to seize the moment. Follow the path of Scottish Widows, a U.K. insurer and Lloyds Banking Group subsidiary, which launched a compelling public awareness campaign informing young women of financial perils in their older years. It even has an app called Beat the Gap.

The point is future generations will all be better off if today's young women make decisions that benefit their long-term financial well-being. That means providing early information that most will not otherwise know. Until it is too late.

Women in their 40s, 50s, or 60s, already established in careers, are locked into decisions that will impact their retirement. And many are still immersed in child-rearing or caring for aging parents. Often both. This is a period of exhaustion not contemplated in "Labour," but true to theme, it's hard to do it all. I have interviewed many women who left their jobs to look after parents, an incredibly generous and loving gift. It's a beautiful part of a shared legacy. But depending on an individual's finances, and expectations of an inheritance often shared with multiple siblings, it comes with a cost that we do not consider.

Sometimes the diseases of old age arrive with indiscriminate timing. One woman learned of terminal diagnoses for her father, mother, and stepfather within a few years. Her dad lived on the West Coast. Her mom and stepfather in southern Ontario. She spent years caring for all three, driving hours to her stepfather's house or flying across the country to visit her dad, all while living on the declining equity from her house, sold in a divorce.

"When my parents got sick, I chose to give them my time. I chose to spend the money that I had from my house and directed my energy toward looking after them," she says. "So, you know,

I'm glad that I was able to do that for them, but it did position me badly, I would say, in the end."

Many single mothers spend money on children or our own well-being, an invaluable investment, but as already discussed this can be expensive and acknowledging personal responsibility for some decisions is empowering.

To recoup that money, many of us work long past the typical retirement age. We joke about Freedom 75, but with the reasonable expectation of a 100-year life, there is a financial blessing in every extra year that a salary pays into a pension. It's also good for the brain and social connections. Of course, it is much easier if you have a job that doesn't require heavy labour.

Once out of the workforce, it can be hard to get back in, and like the woman who cared for her three parents, a decision to take CPP at 60 takes the edge off. However, it is a less-than-stellar long-term strategy. A lot of Canadians do it.

Ideally, we will build retirement savings that enable a comfortable existence for 40 years after the typical retirement age because, with the new longevity, you never know. And don't forget, late-life expenses include more than housing and food. Some will grow fragile, perhaps breaking a hip due to osteoporosis. We can walk and lift weights to stay strong, but no one can predict what is coming. Outside help for bathing, cooking, or eating requires a lot of money.

One of the easiest ways to finance old age is through delayed gratification.

Payments from CPP or Old Age Security are demonstrably higher when we delay taking them until 70. Over a long life, this can provide tens of thousands of additional dollars, if not more.

Of course, not everyone agrees with this approach. There are differing calculations on the age when we will "break even" from delaying such benefits. So, is it worth waiting? Well, that depends on lifespan. Those with a long run sure appreciate it. As always, when it comes to pensions, nuance rules. And there are changes that could help some make better decisions.

Actuary and pension expert Dr. Bonnie-Jeanne MacDonald is on a mission to improve the monetary well-being of older Canadians. If an individual waits until the age of 70, MacDonald says, the monthly payment from CPP will double. But, starting CPP at the age of 60 instead of waiting until 70 would result in the loss of $100,000 over an average lifespan of a typical person Dr. MacDonald says, in research published by the National Institute on Ageing (NIA) where she serves as director of financial security.

A lot of Canadians take CPP as soon as it's available to them, her report says, because after paying into it for decades, they are convinced that an early demise would leave all that money in the system instead of their estate. Most of us will live past the age of 70, when we must start our pension, Dr. MacDonald says. But the possibility of an early death means losing money paid into CPP during decades of work identifies a legitimate unfairness.

With that in mind, here are two worthy recommendations from Dr. MacDonald's research.

To alleviate the fear of loss from an early death, CPP should offer a "pension-back" death benefit to help Canadians benefit from delaying payments until the cut-off age of 70.

This would serve two functions, Dr. MacDonald's report says. Canadians could delay taking the public pension to get more money later. And depending on the age at death, beneficiaries would get the difference in income lost by not collecting at 60. (Once again, nothing related to pensions is simple.)

"This death benefit," MacDonald writes, "would make up the difference between the cumulative amount the participant *actually* received and what they *would* have received had they claimed at age 60. Note that the death benefit is not the entire value of the CPP/QPP benefit; it is only the lost income from delaying benefits."

The second recommendation is basic but clearly important: Improve Canadians' CPP knowledge.

Rather than the quick online process that enables Canadians to register for an early pension with little knowledge of the consequences, Dr. MacDonald says there should be a requirement for a conversation with a reachable Service Canada specialist (in person or by phone) to explain choices and outcomes. A 2023 NIA survey found that just one in seven public pension recipients reported making a "significant effort" to attain knowledge before claiming CPP. Some said they made the decision "without giving it much thought." Interventions that educate, she wrote, could slow the process just enough for people to make an informed decision with lifelong impact.

Improvements such as these make sense. Older people, especially those long retired, cannot easily restart their careers, but tweaks can bring fairness and proper education for those on the precipice, and they can make a difference. Perhaps some are flush with savings when they choose early CPP, but making such decisions with no real knowledge seems cavalier and self-defeating.

We're all playing the odds, but it helps to consider the long game.

• • •

For today's retired women, the *average* payment from Canada's public pension offers grocery money but not much else. In 2024, the average monthly CPP payment for women was $575. Men did considerably better with nearly $800. We have already discussed the reasons for this — including pensions based on male-pattern employment and a long uninterrupted career.

If only there was a way to perpetuate the human species without structural inequity.

Ever so slowly, the outside world might be catching on. When I first wrote about the impoverishment of older women for the *Star* in March 2023, many readers seemed shocked about the existence of this thing called the gender pension gap. Of course, it was well documented in reports such as those from Ontario's Pay Equity Office or the federal Standing Committee on the Status of Women, but the financial lives of older women were not part of the zeitgeist. It was interesting to see the response from readers to that story. It gathered hundreds of online comments, and analytics showed that readership numbers were unexpectedly high. I wrote a lot of articles on serious age-related issues for the *Star*'s Third Act project, and few received so many online hits. Readers sent emotional emails, shocked that women end up living this way. I am told that one woman, a high-powered executive, sobbed when she finished the story. It hits us for different reasons, not just financial. For some, it is loneliness that we fear, debilitating in its own way.

In late 2024, I wrote another piece on the gender pension gap and the lack of affordable housing. Again, readers were deeply engaged. Older women do not often see their lives discussed in the mainstream, but it is my working theory that they welcome the recognition.

At the Pay Equity Office of Ontario, commissioner Kadie Philp believes that, at least in large multinational organizations, a new energy is shifting toward these issues. Leaders are starting to talk about the gender pension gap, Philp says, and pressure for change may be building.

Some of that awareness is emerging, she says, because governments, such as those in Canada, have started analyzing programs through a gender lens, and while that may sound vague, methodologies used to evaluate policies show the bias is real.

The PEO is not an advocacy group. Its role, Philp says, is to bring the issue of wage and retirement equity to the public. Its 2024 report by Dr. Elizabeth Shilton, *Understanding the Gender Pension Gap in Canada*, has, without a doubt, elevated our knowledge of the biases that women face across their working lives.

What matters increasingly are the voices of women.

There is an undeniable case that government policies originating in the *Mad Men* days led to inequities in late life. It's time for a rewrite. And perhaps a 2026 coalition of advocates to elevate the work of actuaries and legal scholars. Yes, women-led organizations have fought for change in the past, with some success, but demographics evolve and the cohort of mid-life women that took on menopause will not enter old age quietly. It was women in their 40s and 50s who shifted the supposedly taboo topic of menopause to a viral social media campaign for better education and medical attention. It's unlikely they will suddenly grow quiet after recognizing what's coming next. They're just really busy and could use the help.

With a focus on the public pension plan, here are a few of many recommendations for change from Dr. Shilton's report for the PEO.

- **Consider a speedier transition to 33 percent of income.** "If gender-based analysis confirms that the pension enhancement will have positive gender effects, women should not have to wait until 2059 to see the full impact of those effects in their pensions."

- **Introduce a one- or two-year COVID-19 drop-out period.** There is a seven-year low-income drop-out allowed for those raising children full-time, meaning the lesser wages won't be counted in the eventual CPP payment. A similar approach would help women who had to the leave the workforce during the pandemic, often for family needs.

- **Reduce the 40 years needed to qualify for full CPP.** Since the average Canadian gets just over half of the maximum benefit, the CPP assumption that most spend four decades in the workforce "does not realistically reflect the careers of average Canadians." Fewer years would benefit all Canadians with an emphasis on women, who spend less time in the workforce due to the "disproportionate distribution of family care work."

- **Conduct timely analysis on pensions and women.** While the federal government has increased its use of "gender-based analysis," it still needs to sharpen its focus on the public pension.

The Gap

Many women won't be seriously affected by the retirement gap. Some say those who are should have worked harder when they had the chance. Or spent less on their kids. And while we must all recognize the impact of our decisions, the warnings about women's retirement income are coming not from sympathetic social justice groups but from large financial organizations.

Mercer, a global consulting firm, has moved beyond the mere identification of the gap. While we know that women are increasingly seeking public sector jobs with good pensions, Mercer researchers are not bullish on the retirement of women entering the workforce today.

"It is tempting to think the gender pension gap only affects older generations," says Mercer principal Lin Shi, "but the reality is that younger women are still on track to face many of the same challenges, unless we actively address them."

"Pay gaps persist," Shi says. "Many women start their careers earning less than their male counterparts, which compounds over time. Caregiving responsibilities remain unequal, leading women to take more career breaks or work part-time, directly reducing their long-term savings. Financial literacy gaps and relatively lower investment confidence may hold many women back from building long-term wealth at the same rate as men."

Among Shi's recommendations are the following:

- Companies could improve access to retirement plans, conduct pay equity reviews, and offer financial education.

- Flexible work policies could allow individuals (more likely to be women) to balance caregiving without sacrificing long-term financial security.

- Governments could offer greater incentives for employers to provide credits in private pension schemes.

"The gender pension gap," Shi says, "will not disappear on its own, and the sooner we address it proactively, the better we can ensure financial security for all generations."

Every year, the Mercer CFA Global Pension Index examines international retirement systems, and a recent version highlighted a problem that's coming for Gen X and millennials: dementia and the defined contribution plan.

My mother, who loved to concoct imaginary names for rock bands, would have said Dementia and the Defined Contribution Plan was a catchy label for a troupe of aging hipster musicians, but seriously, it points to a problem most don't consider. Longevity can outlast cognition.

Defined contributions, Mercer noted, are essentially investment funds that rely on the ever-shifting markets and an owner capable of properly directing its management through sound long-term decisions. It is "important to recognize that cognitive ability declines with age, and it is therefore inappropriate to expect retirees to continue to make these decisions into their 80s and 90s," Mercer's report said.

To mitigate the risk, the report said the defined contribution plan should be "at a minimum, a structured lifetime payment with the potential for a lifetime income guarantee to protect against their longevity risk."

This is not to suggest that all people in their 80s or 90s will live with cognitive decline, but as the defined benefit pensions lose ground to defined contribution plans, it's an advance warning on the need for trusted financial management.

Housing

Where and how will we live in our later years? It is the key to a good long life.

Here is a bit of wisdom from Maytree with its long-established history of social justice research. Housing, it says, plays an outsized role in financial well-being and by extension our physical health.

Many Canadians believe that older adults can simply boost their late-life income by selling one big asset, their house, Maytree reports say. This is not always true, since many are increasingly renters: "The current Canadian housing crisis and ongoing drop in homeownership mean that seniors who do not have the privilege of homeownership may face uncertain living conditions and ever-increasing rental costs."

Even those who own homes may live with uncertainty, as bodies grow fragile or cognitive decline arrives. Where do they go? Retirement homes can cost up to $120,000 a year, which means a lot of people would outlive their money. If one grows vulnerable but wants to age in place, the cost of full-time private nursing care can exceed $10,000 per month.

One of the easiest ways to help people remain healthy and independent is the opportunity provided by NORCs — naturally occurring retirement communities, the condos or apartments with a significant density of older adults. The opportunity to reach so many people — and enable home-care workers to stay busy in one community — makes such good sense it's a wonder Ontario has yet to embrace them.

In a time when governments are trying to save money on long hospital stays, there is a growing collection of data that shows programs and home care brought into a community has a positive impact on the lives of older people and, as the University Health

Network's NORC Innovation Centre found, the lives of front-line workers who are also in short supply.

The NORC concept is increasingly popular, even as a DIY model. In one Toronto condominium, residents recognized the need for outside support when a much older woman, a condo owner, walked outside on a cold winter day in her nightgown and lay in the snow, demanding the concierge leave her to die.

And while it is not technically a NORC, a Halton Region community housing building created intentionally for older residents uses a program similar to American NORCs. Ontario government-funded research into this specific model found fewer and shorter hospitalizations among residents with health chronic conditions, making it increasingly clear that social programs and health supports can help many live in the community.

It's just so practical.

We've already discussed options such as shared rentals promoted by Senior Women Living Together or Quebec's Radical Resthomes. Since these ideas increasingly captivate, related programs could all use a boost from family trusts, charities, or governments. Unfortunately, Canada has a massive deficit in affordable housing, and these small projects, which all have their place, cannot solve the big affordability problem.

The definition of *affordability* also needs to change, says Tim Richter, the housing expert. A greater focus on affordability based on income rather than market rent would help. "In the national housing strategy [of the previous government], the federal government spent billions on what they called affordable housing but it wasn't affordable to anybody," he says.

In Vancouver, even some higher income households could not afford the units being built as part of Canada's earlier housing strategy; the cohort most at risk, Richter says, are older adults.

Given Canada's decades-long drought in the construction of housing, here are solutions from housing experts:

- **Legitimize affordability.** Richter says affordability should focus on rent geared to income.

- **Offer support until housing is built.** The vast majority of people on the wait-lists for subsidized housing are already housed but cannot afford the rent. Richter is calling for a "homelessness prevention housing benefit" for those with the deepest needs, who are spending more than 50 percent of their income on rent.

- **Ramp up social housing construction.** Governments, from Ottawa to the provinces and municipalities, need to work together to quickly and affordably increase social housing units. This includes housing with built-in home-care supports for older adults or younger people with disabilities. Among the 22 percent of Canadian renters who are living in the official definition of "core housing need" (mostly due to unaffordability), many are older adults, often women on a fixed income, he says.

Housing deeply matters to our well-being. We see this in the architectural design of cities. The good ones create space that allows for people of all ages and respects that some will use wheelchairs or walkers. The same goes for apartments with wide doors and walk-in showers.

If older adults are forced to spend much of their income on rent and the rest on food, there is nothing left for life. Somewhere along the way, starting in the late 1980s, governments and taxpayers forgot that building the infrastructure otherwise known as truly affordable homes is a profound investment in public health.

CHAPTER EIGHTEEN

Crystallized Intelligence

"Listen to old women, motherfuckers."

— JULIA LOUIS-DREYFUS

By the time this book is in your hands, I will have spent a few years immersed in the stories of women who have been around for a very long time. By listening to their experiences, their struggle and survival, I am blessed with a pragmatically rich perspective of what is to come.

So, with inspiration from the inimitable Julia Louis-Dreyfus, who offered that sage quote while accepting a Webby Podcast of the Year Award for *Wiser Than Me*, here is some wisdom from Canadian women who came before us.

Plan ahead for housing that will fit life, with all its surprises, in your later years. Ask yourself, How do I want to live when I'm 80? In case of unexpected health problems, will you be able to access support in your home? Start by the time you're 55, as feminist activist Erin Harris says, especially if you are trying to get your name on a wait-list for co-operative housing or other affordable options. In the meantime, Harris says, give away furniture. It is freeing.

For many, life is long, so allow yourself the grace to fail and evolve. Pay attention to the energy people bring to your life, and foster relationships with the good ones, especially women. As Jane Fonda and numerous scientists say, the oxytocin created by female friendships is life-affirming. Also, make younger friends in case you outlive your peers. It happens.

Susan Patricia Staples recommends building a community in your neighbourhood or city so the friends you rely on for emotional sustenance are not a 20-hour drive away. Elizabeth appreciates the value of contentment. Pat Dunn believes in action instead of griping.

Elizabeth saves money for her anticipated entry to the centenarian club by only purchasing what she needs, not what she wants. (It's a process.) Once a year, she splurges on concert tickets with a friend, and they look forward to it for months. Never think about what you can't have, she says, because self-pity wraps us in self-perpetuating misery. For those who complain that nobody notices old people, Elizabeth says, nonsense! Go outside. Walk with your chin up and greet fellow citizens. There are a lot of great people of all ages out there. You're bound to like a few. Get a dog. If you can't get one, say hi to the dogs that pass you on the street. Don't let your body go. You need it! Walk. Lift heavy things.

Listen to young women, too, like Stephanie Hinds who isn't afraid to let go of a man who does not respect her. Why follow societal demands that we must stick it out, no matter how painful a relationship has become? Better to have peace and a home of one's own with a cat sleeping on the computer while you write.

Dr. Paula Rochon reminds us that long life is a privilege. And one that a great many do not receive. So best take care of yourself along the way. Take time to consider your physical and emotional well-being, because it has the potential to impact the way you age. Exercise the body and brain. Create social connections. Spend more time with friends, or rekindle connections from the past.

Stay curious, study a new religion, or get in touch with the rising moon of your inner crone. Listen to Inge Fowlie and allow yourself the opportunity to fall in love. Listen to Inge again and become unafraid of disrobing in front of a good man or whatever good human you desire. Follow your intuition and, if you wish, remain open to the loveliness of new friendship or romance. Love comes in many forms, she says, and they're all good.

Save precious time and take note of red flags in potential relationships because they are always there if we are willing to acknowledge them, however painful. Best to protect oneself against predatory people, those professing love but quietly hoping to finagle a partner's equity, pension, or just live on the cheap. Leanne Kaufman, the president and CEO of RBC Royal Trust, advises against marriage or living common-law without a legally binding prenuptial or cohabitation agreement. These agreements protect your assets in case a partner's ulterior motive is masked by charm. It happens.

Or, as so many women are now doing, enjoy your private space, and should you choose to date, find people with their own home, offering a freedom that can lead to lasting ties.

Susi Bowen and Rick Benson fell in love when she was 71 and he was 65. I interviewed them six years later. As a couple, they are strong, still living apart, still enjoying their time together. Listening to Susi and others who found a later-in-life romance, it seems that other older women are endlessly intrigued by couples of a similar vintage who are delighting in each other's company. When Susi met up with girlfriends she knew from years earlier, before her husband died, they asked a lot of questions about her new man. In polite company, it went unasked, but it seemed as if they were curious about sex.

"When I left the luncheon and one of the gals said to me, 'Just remind me again. What's his name?' So, I said to her, 'His name is Rick Benson. And yes, we have carnal knowledge of each other,'" she says, laughing. "And yeah, it is nice to be touched. It makes you realize you're alive."

CHAPTER NINETEEN

The Denouement

Pat

What should be clear by now is that Pat found a landlord willing to rent a modest brick home, with a walkout basement, in Peterborough to three older women. It's a few blocks from Costco, her least favourite store. The houses on her street have narrow yards, and the cars in neighbours' driveways are rusty, like hers.

Pat still misses Dave. She would have liked a relationship with another man, but at least for a time, that part of her life is over. She values her female friends. When the woman who lives on the upper level was hospitalized, Pat visited her near daily. They'd talk in the hospital room, just like they talked at home.

"I love her," Pat says. "Like a friend. She is important to me."

Their home has a moppish dog who stays close to Pat, following on her heels as she walks down the hallway to her bedroom, where there is just enough room for a desk holding a computer and piles of paper. This is the energy centre of Senior Women Living Together. Photos of Dave and Pat are framed in a dining room hutch that acts as a bookcase. One image shows the couple at a black-tie event, two beautiful tall people laughing.

Pat often spends 12 hours a day at her desk, talking online or in Zoom meetings, which are better than phone calls due to her partial hearing loss. By early 2025, Senior Women Living Together had helped more than 60 women find roommates and affordable rent.

To be honest, Pat says, it isn't always easy, helping people find matches. A lot of women connect through the SWLT Facebook site for emotional support, seeking a place to vent and a sympathetic ear but do not ultimately take the plunge into shared living. For those in big cities, it's next to impossible to find an apartment with enough bedrooms at a price that makes shared renting worthwhile. Some, like Elizabeth, who once considered moving to a more affordable city, decide not to leave their community, reluctant to start over once again.

Today, Senior Women Living Together has a five-year plan with a new focus on outreach for Ontario women at risk of homelessness. The group will, of course, carry on with its core purpose, creating a space for women to match with potential roommates. One of the next-stage goals, Pat says, is the support of similar SWLTs across Canada and the creation of partnerships with non-profit housing providers, such as WoodGreen Community Services in Toronto, that sometimes offer her members two- or three-bedroom rentals that have no takers.

As the years pass, Pat's advocacy grows. She's trying to raise awareness about the financial distress of older women. When she speaks of society's apparent disinterest in women or older people in general, her voice hardens. Where was the collective outrage, she asks, when thousands of nursing home residents, most of whom were women, died during the pandemic?

The women she supports through SWLT, particularly those with little money, tell her they would rather have medical assistance in dying than end up in a nursing home. The reality is that often it is these women, with little money and diminished health, who spend their final years in a hospital or long-term care home. After all the labour performed throughout their lives, the husbands loved, children raised, houses made homes, what does that say about the value we place on women once this work is done?

As it happens, Pat had a health scare in the spring of 2024. Suddenly short of breath, she got herself to the hospital where doctors found blood clots throughout her lungs. In the following months, Pat had numerous appointments with specialists trying to uncover the cause. Doctors found nothing wrong, she says proudly, with any part of her body.

And yet now, in her mid-70s, Pat feels the arthritis in her knees and hips. She and her two housemates are preparing for the next life phase — a rental house with no stairs or only a few stairs at most.

In Pat's old life, the world of sailing, there is a truism about finding one's destination. Sailors learn, over time, that navigation relies not just on winds but an awareness that below the ocean's surface hidden currents will pull a boat off course. With the experience of time, a sailor will flow with the current until it eases and, tacking starboard, fill the sails for a new way forward.

That's why Pat and her housemates are starting early, looking for a new, affordable place to land.

Susan

Knee surgery is supposed to be routine. Susan's surgery may have gone well, but her blood pressure was so low that she didn't go home. She stayed in her hospital bed, a sedentary experience that, she says, inflamed her sore back; neuropathy emerged in her feet, a painful tingling she had thus far avoided, that was probably related to her diabetes. It was agony. This is the kind of ill health she feared, which can lead to a wheelchair and a physical decline that she does not want to live with. She would prefer medical assistance in dying over suffering like this for the remainder of her years.

It was with a bleary heart that Susan greeted the summer of 2024. In less than stellar physical condition, all the excitement for her road trip hovered in a cloud of frustration. June passed. So did July. By August, Susan concluded that she would not survive the winter in her apartment without nomading, so she organized the supplies in her van and said goodbye to her son who knows better than to try to stop his mother.

That first day on the road, Susan stayed focused on her destination — the farm in Nova Scotia. Usually, it takes five or so days to get there. This time she held tight to the steering wheel, flying along the Trans-Canada Highway through Montreal, past the small towns of eastern Quebec. Just before the city lines of Edmundston, New Brunswick, as the August sunlight dimmed, Susan pulled into her favourite campground at le parc provincial de la République. It's clean, the park wardens are always friendly, and best of all, the seniors' rate was $25 a night. Susan's favourite spot is in the back, far from the sound of traffic. She parked near the trees and ate a packaged meal, a tin of tuna with a few crackers. Using her walker to move around her van, Susan lifted the hatchback to give herself extra breathing room overnight, opened the sliding side door, and slowly climbed inside, settling on the foam bed, her head facing the rear of the van. It always surprised her to see photos of the set-ups used by women in the car life Facebook group, since most slept with their heads pointed toward the front of the vehicle. The back-facing position may have seemed vulnerable, but to Susan it felt blissful, like she was close to nature.

Sleep came fast. So did the morning. Sometimes she lingers at the campsite but today, Susan felt the need to get on the road. She had a shower, washed out a few thermoses in the campground kitchen, stopped for a coffee and bagel at the local Tim Hortons, and started driving. Edmundston was halfway to her friends' farm in Pictou County, near the Northumberland Strait. She hadn't done a one-day drive like yesterday since her early 60s, long before she ever considered life with a knee replacement and neuropathy.

That night, Susan turned onto the long lane that leads to the farm and parked her van in the usual spot near the house, in the circular driveway under the huge old maple trees. This is one of her happy places, a big old home with space for visiting families of the two women who live there, partners for years.

Two days later, relaxing at the backyard swimming pool, Susan's friend called out, "What's that thing on the back of your leg?" Susan had no idea. She felt nothing. Hadn't seen anything. But something *was* on her calf, and Susan's friend was sufficiently disturbed that she took a photo, which looked like stage five melanoma on Google Images. Susan drove to the QEII Cancer Centre in Halifax where a doctor referred her to the dermatology department. On the referral form, Susan read the words "possible melanoma."

Well, that was unexpected. The next morning Susan packed up her van, hugged her friends goodbye, and, as quickly as she came, drove back to Ottawa where her doctors diagnosed not cancer, thankfully, but a small and extremely deep diabetic ulcer, one that required three visits a week from a wound nurse, who changed the specialized dressings. And yet it would not heal.

It is the physical changes from aging that Susan struggles with the most. She saw herself as powerful, through her 50s and 60s, her best decades really, when she was comfortable with herself and handled whatever came her way. Somewhere along the arc of years, her body started to change. This loss of control, it was infuriating. And scary. In the fall of 2024, Susan swears more, dropping F-bombs over this little hole in her leg that is so deleterious to her Zen.

In her dreams, Susan is driving south to her women friends in Pennsylvania, but she cannot leave Ottawa until those visits with the nurse are done. Just like last January in the hospital, she is trapped by her body. As December ends, Susan considers heading out, but she is about to become a first-time grandmother so the desire for travel competes with this new urge to help her son and his wife, although given her reliance on a walker, she isn't sure how much help she will be. She's almost afraid now that her love for the baby will overpower her desire for the road.

Driving in her van to parts planned and unknown fills two needs in opposition to each other and yet Susan can't live without either. Nomading takes her to friends, emotionally and intellectually profound relationships that sustain her during long winter nights alone in her apartment, and it also offers aloneness, watching towns flash by and sitting on the beaches of Maine with the ocean.

Nomading nourishes the soul, as Susan says, and as her health changes, stealing her freedom, she will enter the darkest months of winter feeling empty, hoping that new life, a baby, will bring peace so when the snow melts in the spring, she won't be forsaken by her body. Not this time.

Elizabeth

In her tiny basement studio, Elizabeth manages.

Rent goes up every year, but so far she has no plans to make any changes, not yet. In her mid-80s, Elizabeth is hoping her savings will survive what she expects will be a very long life. Her biggest birthday is less than 20 years away, and while anything can happen, Elizabeth will likely become a centenarian, so she practises financial pragmatism.

She takes her dog to the park for the morning meet-up with her walking crew, who are dear friends now. One day, as she bounded out of the woods and began her march along the sidewalk, a woman in her 20s stopped her, complimenting Elizabeth on her outfit. She was wearing baggy jeans, a denim jacket, and a beloved sweater knit for her by a friend, balanced by her trusty Doc Martens. She smiled all the way home.

When she's not walking in the forest, playing wind instruments in a band remains her place of joy. No one is happier than a bunch of people who get together and make music, she says. At home, Elizabeth tends to potted plants that wouldn't survive on the sunlight provided by her one window except they, too, found a way to carry on, buoyed by tiny artificial lights.

When her old car stopped working in the fall of 2024, she called her financial advisor and asked if she should pay for repairs or buy a different one. A man of few words, his advice remains the same on all expenditure queries: "If it's a need, not just a want." As it turned out, the repair bill would have hit $10,000, so her mechanic found her a little jalopy for $7,800. If it, too, becomes unaffordable, Elizabeth says she will use public transit.

For now, Elizabeth, Pat, and Susan are keeping their cars, just in case.

Acknowledgements

This book would not have happened without the women who shared their stories with me, speaking of unexpected financial hardship, love, loss, and dreams for the future. From the older women to those who are young, their perspectives gave life to a book focused on the complicated relationship between longevity and the gender pension gap in unaffordable times. Pat, Susan, and Elizabeth offered secrets and knowledge, based on decades of hindsight, while Stephanie offered the perspective of a young woman facing a world vastly changed.

I am also deeply grateful to those who, having spent years focused on issues such as pensions or women's health, offered their expertise. This includes the geriatrician and scientist Dr. Paula Rochon, for her thoughtful insight into women's well-being, and the legal scholar and author Dr. Elizabeth Shilton, whose report on pay gaps and pensions for the Pay Equity Office of Ontario became a reassuring reference. Whenever new questions arose, and they always did, Dr. Shilton's work offered the answer.

My book editor, Pia Singhal of ECW Press, recognized the value of what initially must have seemed like an opaque concept, and our early creative discussions led to deeper narratives on older women, the heart of the book. Samantha Haywood, literary agent and president of Transatlantic Agency, saw the promise from the start, and I am grateful for her very smart representation.

I'd like to thank copy editor Crissy Boylan and proofreader Kathryn Lane, who brought an elegant touch to their suggestions and, all the ECW staff, Victoria Cozza, Emily Ferko, Cassie Smyth, Samantha Chin, and Jennifer Gallinger, who give life to books and moved this one along with such enthusiasm.

The *Toronto Star*, where I work full-time, has a strong commitment to storytelling focused on the lives of older adults. Our publisher, Jordan Bitove, created the *Star*'s Third Act Project to challenge traditional views on aging and our editor-in-chief, Nicole MacIntyre, is the creative force, launching new ways to elevate longevity journalism. And, much gratitude to JP Fozo, the *Star*'s executive producer of multimedia, for the unrelenting enthusiasm he brought to the stories on older adults and the podcast I host, How to Live to 100 or Die Trying. I have been part of the Third Act since its inception and the experience deepened my understanding of what it means to prepare for a good life in our much older years. Hopefully, it does the same for readers. Exposing inequities to create change is the goal of the *Star*'s journalism and, most definitely, the goal of this book.

Speaking of the *Toronto Star*, I'd like to thank my friend Kevin Donovan for his role as a sounding board for my book, over a glass of wine or text. Our inevitable disagreements made ideas sharper. And, as a testament to the benefits of a new challenge, I am now writing about politics at the *Star*'s Queen's Park bureau.

My colleagues, Robert Benzie, Martin Regg Cohn, Kris Rushowy, and Rob Ferguson, have all offered incredible support.

There are so many others who helped along the way, including Laura Tamblyn Watts, who gladly spoke about older women and sexuality, which, I discovered, still seems to be a taboo topic, although not among a lot of older women. Jen Recknagal, of the UHN's NORC Innovation Centre, connected me to wonderful women who are creating new housing projects. I appreciate the support of Margaret Geare of the Retired Women Teachers of Ontario, who spoke about the RWTO's advocacy for long-term care improvements and introduced me to women who found late-life romance. I appreciate the time and wisdom of Mary Connell, the ever-insightful former public nurse whose purse is always full of emergency supplies. And, Allan Parkin, of the National Yacht Club, whose lesson on the intangibles of sailing, found a place in my book.

Finally, on a personal note, I'd like to thank my two sons, Daniel and David, who listened to my stories of the women in this book, often with emotion. Now adults with busy careers, my boys have grown into kind men. And as a reminder of the feminist economist's advice to pick your partners well, a shout-out to my brilliant and hard-working daughter-in-law, Stephanie, who trains for Iron Man competitions while her husband, the guy who loves his male-dominated workplace, happily does all the meal planning, grocery shopping, and cooking. This is shared labour.

Notes

Introduction

- *Centenarians are one of Canada's fastest*: "A Portrait of Canada's Growing Population Aged 85 and Older from the 2021 Census," Statistics Canada, April 27, 2022, online.
- *Women in their 80s, such as actor and activist Jane Fonda*: Jane Fonda and Lily Tomlin, "A Hilarious Celebration of Lifelong Female Friendship," TEDWomen, May 2015, online.
- *Statistically speaking, it is the men who depart first*: "Life Expectancy and Other Elements of the Complete Life Table, Single-Year Estimates, Canada, All Provinces Except Prince Edward Island," Statistics Canada, December 4, 2024, online.
- *For Canadians born in 1901*: Robert Bourbeau, Jacques Légaré, and Valérie Émond, *New Birth Cohort Life Tables for Canada and Quebec, 1801–1991*. Statistics Canada, 1997, online.
- *As Dr. Rochon explains*: Paula A. Rochon et al., "Polypharmacy, Inappropriate Prescribing, and Deprescribing in Older People: Through a Sex and Gender Lens," *The Lancet Healthy Longevity* 2, no. 5 (2021): e290–e300, online.
- *Today, the sheer economic power*: Administration for Community Living, "2023 Profile of Older Americans," U.S. Department of Health and Human Services, May 2024, online.
- *This may explain why longitudinal data*: Sian Cain, "Women Are Happier

Without Children or a Spouse, Says Happiness Expert," *The Guardian*, May 25, 2019, online.

- *But if solitude turns to isolation*: Rachel Savage et al., "Loneliness Epidemic Among Older Adults in Canada," Women's Age Lab, Women's College Hospital, March 2024.
- *To sharpen the pain of loneliness*: Elizabeth Shilton, *Understanding the Gender Pension Gap in Canada*. Pay Equity Office, May 2024, online.
- *A prospect worsened by Canada's desperate lack of affordable housing*: Statistics Canada, "Housing Challenges Related to Affordability, Adequacy, Condition and Discrimination, August 2 to September 15, 2024," *The Daily*, November 19, 2024, online.
- *To be fair to Canadian policy-makers*: Shilton, *Understanding the Gender Pension Gap*; Statistics Canada, "Canadian Income Survey, 2023," *The Daily*, May 1, 2025, online.
- *Most of the women I interviewed for this book*: Garson Hunter and Miguel Sanchez, "Child and Family Poverty in Saskatchewan: November 2017," Social Policy Research Centre, University of Regina, 2020, online; Priyanka Sibal and Dennis Raphael, "What Is Behind the Fluctuations in Seniors' Poverty Rates in Canada from 1976–2019?" *Canadian Review of Social Policy* 82 (2022): 58–82, online.
- *Even if salary disparities ended tomorrow, the benefits*: Shilton, *Understanding the Gender Pension Gap*.
- *Old age, writ large, is coming*: Karine Leclerc, *The Poverty Rate and Low-Income Situation of Older Persons in Canada: An Intersectional Analysis*. Statistics Canada, Centre for Gender, Diversity and Inclusion Statistics, December 4, 2024, online.
- *I published a story in early 2023 that examined the struggles of women*: Moira Welsh, "They Had Families, Worked Hard and Grew Old. Now They Face Their Final Years in Poverty. Why Are We Failing Older Women in Canada?" *Toronto Star*, March 16, 2023, online.
- *There is a painful truth in acknowledging*: N. Iciaszczyk, G. Gallant, T. Bronstein, A. Brierley, and S.K. Sinha. *Perspectives on Growing Older in Canada: The 2024 NIA Ageing in Canada Survey*. National Institute on Ageing, Toronto Metropolitan University, 2024.
- *By the early 2030s, nearly one in four Canadians*: National Institute on Ageing and Environics Institute for Survey Research, *Perspectives on Growing Older in Canada: The 2022 NIA Ageing in Canada Survey*. National Institute on Ageing, Toronto Metropolitan University, 2022, online.

- *In two decades, we will enter our potentially frail years*: "A Portrait of Canada's Growing Population," Statistics Canada.
- *For the icing on the statistical cake*: Email to author from Statistics Canada, Media Hotline, January 24, 2024.
- *In the United States, the number*: Katherine Schaeffer, "U.S. Centenarian Population Is Projected to Quadruple over the Next 30 Years," Pew Research Center, January 9, 2024, online.
- *Canada's gender pension gap was 22 percent*: OECD, *Towards Improved Retirement Savings Outcomes for Women*. OECD Publishing, 2021.
- *Pay Equity Office of Ontario puts the pension gap at 17 percent*: Shilton, *Understanding the Gender Pension Gap*.

Chapter One: Susan, Pat, and Elizabeth

- *with more than 80,000 Ontarians known to be homeless*: "Municipalities Under Pressure: The Human and Financial Cost of Ontario's Homelessness Crisis," Association of Municipalities of Ontario, January 2025, online.
- *It's often higher for racialized women*: Sheila Block, Grace-Edward Galabuzi, and Hayden King, *Colour-Coded Retirement: An Intersectional Analysis of Retirement Income and Savings in Canada*. Canadian Centre for Policy Alternatives, June 2021, online.
- *Canada's gender pension gap has not narrowed*: Elizabeth Shilton, *Understanding the Gender Pension Gap in Canada*. Pay Equity Office, May 2024, online.
- *In 2024, Canada had 2.4 million men over the age of 70*: "Population Estimates on July 1, by Age and Gender," Statistics Canada, September 9, 2024, online.
- *There is research on aging and older lesbians*: "Labour and Economic Characteristics of Lesbian, Gay and Bisexual People in Canada," Statistics Canada, October 4, 2022, online.
- *not to mention the challenges faced in nursing homes*: Ashley Flanagan and Celeste Pang, *Coming Out and Coming In to Living with Dementia*. National Institute on Ageing, 2022.
- *In the mid-1980's, at the age of 42*: Moira Welsh, "Older Women in Canada Are Facing a Heavy Burden of Poverty. A New Plan Could Be a Start," *Toronto Star*, April 4, 2023.
- *In 2023, the average cost of raising a child*: "How Much Do Canadian Families Spend Raising a Child?" Statistics Canada, November 30, 2023, online.

- *One legal expert has noted*: Lisa Gelman, "I Spent My Life Paying for All My Children's Expenses. Are They Obligated to Help Me Now That I'm Old?" *Toronto Star*, December 9, 2024, online.
- *Canada Pension Plan and Quebec Pension Plan*: "Canada Pension Plan: Pensions and Benefits Monthly Amounts 2025," Government of Canada, July 2, 2025, online.
- *Old Age Security*: "Old Age Security Payment Amounts: Maximum Payments and Income Thresholds — July to September 2025," Government of Canada, August 27, 2025, online.
- *Guaranteed Income Supplement*: "Guaranteed Income Supplement — Allowance," Government of Canada, August 25, 2025, online.

Chapter Two: The CEO

- *compared to 50 years ago, the overall number of Canadians*: "Pensions: The Ups and Downs of Pension Coverage in Canada," Statistics Canada, October 8, 2024, online.
- *Compared to men, women are more likely*: "Alzheimer's Awareness Month," Statistics Canada, January 12, 2024, online.
- *With the exception of early onset dementia*: Canadian Institute for Health Information, *Dementia in Canada*. CIHI, 2018.
- *While Statistics Canada notes some decline in dementia*: "Alzheimer's Awareness Month," Statistics Canada.
- *current numbers show that after the age of 85, one in four*: *Navigating the Path Forward for Dementia in Canada: The Landmark Study, Report #1*. Alzheimer Society Canada, 2022, online.
- *And in 20 years, the number of Canadians*: "A Portrait of Canada's Growing Population Aged 85 and Older from the 2021 Census," Statistics Canada, April 27, 2022, online.
- *only 48 percent of Canadians have a will*: Natalie Iciaszczyk and Samir K. Sinha, *Where There's a Will, There's a Way: Canadian Perspectives on Estate Planning*. National Institute on Ageing, Toronto Metropolitan University, 2023, online.

Chapter Four: Elizabeth

- *Social loneliness*: Rachel Savage et al., "Loneliness Epidemic Among Older Adults in Canada," Women's Age Lab, Women's College Hospital, March 2024.

Chapter Five: A Few Good Girlfriends

- *On her podcast* Wiser Than Me: Julia Louis-Dreyfus, host, *Wiser Than Me*, podcast, season 1, episode 1, "Julia Gets Wise with Jane Fonda," Lemonada, April 11, 2023, online.
- *Years ago, in a studio set up for a TEDWomen Talk*: Jane Fonda and Lily Tomlin, "A Hilarious Celebration of Lifelong Female Friendship," TEDWomen, May 2015, online.
- *Aloneness has a profound impact on people in their teens and 20s*: Laura Rodger, Natalie Iciaszczyk, and Samir K. Sinha, *Understanding Social Isolation and Loneliness Among Older Canadians and How to Address It*. National Institute on Ageing, Toronto Metropolitan University, 2022, online.
- *These conditions hurt emotionally, but physically they bring a risk*: Nathan M. Stall, Rachel D. Savage, and Paula A. Rochon, "Loneliness in Older Adults," *CMAJ* 191, no. 17, (April 29, 2019): E476, online.
- *Dr. Vivek H. Murthy made it his mission*: Julianne Holt-Lunstad, ed., *Our Epidemic of Loneliness and Isolation: The U.S. Surgeon General's Advisory on the Healing Effects of Social Connection and Community*. Office of the U.S. Surgeon General, 2023, online.
- *According to WHO statistics*: WHO Commission on Social Connection, *From Loneliness to Social Connection: Charting a Path to Healthier Societies*. World Health Organization, 2025, online.
- *Research tells us that people who live with a dog*: M.W. Gmeiner, and A. Gschwandtner. "The Value of Pets: The Quantifiable Impact of Pets on Life Satisfaction," *Social Indicators Research* 178 (225): 185–223, online.
- *a 2021 study by the RAND Corporation*: Brad Stulberg, "Extended Loneliness Can Make You More Vulnerable to Extremist Views," *Time*, November 3, 2022, online; Ryan Andrew Brown, Todd C. Helmus, Rajeev Ramchand, Alina I. Palimaru, Sarah Weilant, Ashley L. Rhoades, and Liisa Hiatt, "What Do Former Extremists and Their Families Say About Radicalization and Deradicalization in America?" RAND Corporation, research brief RB-A1071-1, June 25, 2021, online.
- *Membership in extremist groups undoubtedly lands*: Alexa Mikhail, "Depression Is Costing the Global Economy a 'Profound' $1 Trillion per Year, Warns U.S. Surgeon General," *Fortune Well*, December 4, 2023, online.
- *The United Kingdom created a Ministry of Loneliness*: Liming Li, Ludovico Carrino, Erica Reinhard, and Mauricio Avendano, "Has the UK Campaign to End Loneliness Reduced Loneliness and Improved Mental Health in Older Age? A Difference-in-Differences Design,"

The American Journal of Geriatric Psychiatry 32, no. 3 (March 2024): 358–372, online.

- *Nearly one in five aged 65 and older reported feeling*: "A Look at Loneliness Among Seniors," Statistics Canada, November 6, 2023, online.
- *Those who fared the worst*: "A Look at Loneliness," Statistics Canada.
- *In Ontario, the Office of the Chief Coroner says*: Stephanie, Solicitor General, Ontario, Suicide Data Tables. Received by Moira Welsh, July 18, 2024.
- *Pension and RRSP facts*: Statistics Canada, "Pension Plans in Canada, as of January 1, 2023," *The Daily*, August 29, 2024, online.

Chapter Six: The Millennial

- *a discussion on the growing desire to live alone*: Stephanie Hinds, "Linda Evangelista Is the Latest Proudly Single Woman," Lainey Gossip, November 28, 2023, online; Decca Aitkenhead, "Linda Evangelista: 'I Don't Blame Myself Any More,'" *The Sunday Times*, November 26, 2023, online.
- *Stephanie also noted Whoopi Goldberg's comments*: Ana Marie Cox, "Whoopi Goldberg Wants to Make You Feel Better," *The New York Times Magazine*, September 4, 2016, online.
- *Among Canadian women aged 75 and older*: "Census Family Status and Household Living Arrangements, Household Type of Person, Age Group and Gender: Canada, Provinces and Territories, Census Metropolitan Areas and Census Agglomerations," Statistics Canada, July 13, 2022, online.
- *The long-term impact of relationship toxicity*: Matthew Solan, "Prolonged Stress May Increase the Risk of Death from Cancer," *Harvard Health Publishing*, January 1, 2023, online.
- *After Stephanie raises the topic of men with narcissistic tendencies*: Sheenie Ambardar, "Narcissistic Personality Disorder," *Medscape*, March 24, 2025, online; Brindusa Vanta and Michael Quinn, "Understanding Cluster B Personality Disorders," MentalHealth.com, May 17, 2025, online.
- *As Stephanie wrote in her October 2023 column*: Stephanie Hinds, "Maren Morris's Surprise Move," Lainey Gossip, October 18, 2023, online.

Chapter Seven: Susan

- *This number does not account for the hidden homeless*: J. Donaldson, D. Wang, C. Escamilla, and A. Turner, *Municipalities Under Pressure: The Human and Financial Cost of Ontario's Homelessness Crisis*. HelpSeeker Technologies, 2025, online.

- *Earlier data, from the 2021 Canadian Housing Survey*: Marc-Antoine Dionne, Christine Laporte, Jonathan Loeppky, and Alexander Miller, *A Review of Canadian Homelessness Data, 2023*. Statistics Canada, 2023, online.
- *The U.S. National Homelessness Law Center says car life is dangerous*: National Law Center on Homelessness and Poverty, *No Safe Place: The Criminalization of Homelessness in U.S. Cities*. National Law Center on Homelessness and Poverty, 2019, online.

Chapter Eight: The Cars

- *According to the Online Etymology Dictionary*: "Nomad," Online Etymology Dictionary, online.
- *Her most famous photograph is called* Migrant Mother: Sarah Pruitt, "The Real Story Behind the 'Migrant Mother,'" History, May 8, 2020, online.
- *With little left, many held onto their vehicles*: Jessica Bruder, *Nomadland: Surviving America in the Twenty-First Century*. W.W. Norton, 2018.
- *In a 2023 paper, Pruss argued*: Graham J. Pruss, "Homes Without Homes: An Ethno-Archeology of Vehicle Residency in Public Parking," *Human Organization* 82, no. 2 (2023): 153–168, online.
- *A National Homelessness Law Center survey of 187 cities*: National Law Center on Homelessness and Poverty, *No Safe Place: The Criminalization of Homelessness in U.S. Cities*. National Law Center on Homelessness and Poverty, 2019, online.
- *At the peak is Bob Wells*: Bob Wells, @cheapRVliving, YouTube, online.
- *With a growing number of Americans*: Teresa Ghilarducci, "Nothing Beautiful About 21% Cuts to Social Security," *Forbes*, June 1, 2025, online; Maya Brownstein, "Medicaid Cuts: What's at Stake," Harvard T.H. Chan School of Public Health, June 5, 2025, online.
- *It cites research that estimates*: Pruss, "Homes Without Homes."
- *In 2022, Canada's gender pension gap*: How to Fix the Gender Pension Gap. Mercer, 2024, online.

Chapter Nine: Pat

- *Examining the ability to pay for certain necessities*: Michael Mendelson, Geranda Notten, Richard Matern, and Sofia Seer, *Poverty in Canada Through a Deprivation Lens*. Food Banks Canada, 2024, online.

Chapter Ten: The Warning

- *This is a striking improvement*: Statistics Canada, "Low-Income Statistics of Older Women and Men, 1976 to 2022," *The Daily*, December 4, 2024, online.
- *Seemingly endless streams of data on poverty*: Karine Leclerc, *The Poverty Rate and Low-Income Situation of Older Persons in Canada: An Intersectional Analysis*. Centre for Gender, Diversity and Inclusion Statistics, Statistics Canada, December 2024, online.
- *In 2022, the median income (after tax) for male and female*: Email to author from Statistics Canada Media Hot Line, February 28, 2025.
- *Dr. Elizabeth Shilton, a legal scholar, author, and pension expert*: Elizabeth Shilton, *Understanding the Gender Pension Gap in Canada*. Pay Equity Office, May 2024, online.
- *The contrast in retirement income between men and women*: Shilton, *Understanding the Gender Pension Gap*.
- *Canada's private workplace pension system*: Elizabeth J. Shilton, *Empty Promises: Why Workplace Pension Law Doesn't Deliver Pensions*. McGill-Queen's University Press, 2016, 1.
- *Canada's first company pension launched in 1874*: Shilton, *Empty Promises*, 18.
- *The first province to act*: Shilton, *Empty Promises*, 67.
- *The legislation would not come into force*: Shilton, *Empty Promises*, 66.
- *While Ontario successfully killed*: Shilton, *Empty Promises*, 67.
- *In the background of that debate*: Shilton, *Understanding the Gender Pension Gap*, 32; Shilton, *Empty Promises*, 66, 67.
- *Instead of replacing a substantial portion*: "Canada Pension Plan Enhancement," Government of Canada, online.
- *In the 1960s, the public pension was deemed mandatory*: Shilton, *Empty Promises*, 67.
- *To justify such a small payout*: Shilton, *Empty Promises*, 67.
- *Politicians (men) raised their voices*: Shilton, *Understanding the Gender Pension Gap*.
- *Policy makers responsible for the design*: Shilton, *Understanding the Gender Pension Gap*.
- *Survivors' pensions were a "partial solution"*: Shilton, *Understanding the Gender Pension Gap*.
- *Survivor benefits for couples in same-sex relationships*: Shilton, *Understanding the Gender Pension Gap*.

- *It took another nine years for a Supreme Court of Canada*: "Ottawa 'Discriminates' in Same-Sex Pension Payments: Court," *CBC News*, March 1, 2007.
- *In the 1970s, as two-income households*: Shilton, *Understanding the Gender Pension Gap*.
- *In 2021, the federal government announced*: "Toward $10-a-Day: An Early Learning and Child Care Backgrounder," Employment and Social Development Canada, online.
- "*large gaps remain in labour market*": Zohra Jamasi, Sabrina Afroz, Jay Park, and Eklavya Jain, *Women in Ontario's Labour Market: Progress, Challenges and Potential Impacts of $10 a Day Child Care*. Financial Accountability Office of Ontario, 2023, online.
- "*The larger wage gap at older ages reflects*": Jamasi, Afroz, Park, and Jain, *Women in Ontario's Labour Market*.
- *In 2023, Canada had 20.2 million actively working adults*: Statistics Canada, "Labour Force Survey, December 2022," *The Daily*, June 1, 2023, online.
- *9.6 million adult women*: Statistics Canada, "Pension Plans in Canada, as of January 1, 2024."
- *of the 10.6 million men who worked*: Statistics Canada, "Pension Plans in Canada, as of January 1, 2024."
- *The lower numbers for men are due*: "Pensions: The Ups and Downs of Pension Coverage in Canada," Statistics Canada, October 8, 2024, online.
- *Two-thirds of the 7.2 million*: Statistics Canada, "Pension Plans in Canada, as of January 1, 2024," *The Daily*, June 6, 2025, online.
- *Less compelling*: Statistics Canada, "Pension Plans in Canada, as of January 1, 2024"; Statistics Canada, "Pension Plans in Canada, as of January 1, 2021," *The Daily*, July 18, 2022, online.
- *Given the hiring spree*: Catherine Morrison, "Number of Federal Public Service Jobs Could Drop by Almost 60,000, Report Predicts," The Canadian Press, July 24, 2025, online.
- *Many Canadians aged 50*: Natalie Iciaszczyk, Gabrielle Gallant, Talia Bronstein, Alyssa Brierley, and Samir Sinha, *Perspectives on Growing Older in Canada: The 2024 NIA Ageing in Canada Survey*. National Institute on Ageing, Toronto Metropolitan University, 2024, online.
- *And yet the FAO reports that more women*: Jamasi, Afroz, Park, and Jain, *Women in Ontario's Labour Market*.

Chapter Eleven: Pat

- *Between 1997 and 2000*: United States General Accounting Office, Drugs Withdrawn from Market, January 19, 2001, online.
- *Heart disease and stroke*: "Women's Risk Factors," Heart and Stroke Foundation of Canada, online.
- *Almost two-thirds*: Andrew E. Budson, "Why Are Women More Likely to Develop Alzheimer's Disease?" *Harvard Health Publishing*, January 20, 2022, online.
- *Women provide two-thirds of dementia care*: Statistics Canada, "Differences in the Characteristics of Caregivers and Caregiving Arrangements of Canadians, 2018," *The Daily*, January 14, 2022, online.

Chapter Twelve: The Doctor

- *The knowledge gaps persist*: "Healthcare Revolutionized 2030: Women's College Hospital Strategic Plan," Women's College Hospital, 2024, online.
- *One of the challenges of research*: "Thalidomide," Science Museum, December 11, 2019, online.
- *If taken early in pregnancy*: "MotherToBaby Fact Sheets," Organization of Teratology Information Specialists (OTIS), February 2023, online.
- *The U.S. National Institutes of Health*: "History of Women's Participation in Clinical Research," National Institutes of Health Office of Research on Women's Health, April 24, 2024, online.
- "*In 1938, DES*": Alina Yakerson, "Women in Clinical Trials: A Review of Policy Development and Health Equity in the Canadian Context," *International Journal for Equity in Health* 18, no. 56 (2019), online.
- *By the early 1990s, in the U.S. and Canada*: Kirsten Bibbins-Domingo and Alex Helman, eds., *Improving Representation in Clinical Trials and Research: Building Research Equity for Women and Underrepresented Groups*. National Academies Press, 2022.
- *The U.S. ban on premenopausal women in clinical trials*: Bibbins-Domingo and Helman, eds., *Improving Representation.*
- *In 2019, the NIH adopted an "inclusion across lifespan" policy*: "Grants and Funding," National Institutes of Health, online.
- *But, in early 2025, with a new federal government in power:* Daniel Wiessner and Nate Raymond, "Judge Deems Trump's National Institutes of Health Grant Cuts Illegal," Reuters, 16 June 2025, online.
- *The CIHR says it has worked internationally*: CIHR Institute of Gender and Health, *Research Priority Plan 2024–2029: Strengths to Solutions:*

Advancing Sex and Gender Science for Healthy Futures. Canadian Institutes of Health Research, 2024, online.

- *In one example of biological sex differences*: CIHR Institute of Gender and Health, *Science Is Better with Sex and Gender: Strategic Plan 2018–2023*. Canadian Institutes of Health Research, 2018, online.
- *Cardiovascular disease is now noted for distinctions*: CIHR Institute of Gender and Health, *Science Is Better with Sex and Gender*.
- *That strategy requires*: CIHR Institute of Gender and Health, *Science Is Better with Sex and Gender*.
- *Crash-test dummies might be the most relatable example of bias*: Caroline Criado Perez, *Invisible Women: Data Bias in a World Designed for Men*. Abrams Press, 2019.
- *Women and older adults being excluded from clinical trials*: Women's Age Lab, "Women at the Forefront of Aging in Canada: Challenging the Status Quo," Women's College Hospital, 2024, online.
- *How many of us, she says, sat behind a desk*: Qing Meng, Muh-Shi Lin, and I-Shiang Tzeng, "Relationship Between Exercise and Alzheimer's Disease: A Narrative Literature Review," *Frontiers in Neuroscience* 14 (March 25, 2020): 131, online.
- *A growing body of evidence*: Meng, Lin, and Tzeng, "Relationship Between Exercise and Alzheimer's Disease."
- *Affordable community-based housing with those extra services*: Moira Welsh, "Her Pension Wasn't Enough to Cover Toronto Rent. Then She Found a Lifeline in a Different Kind of Housing," *Toronto Star*, December 24, 2024, online.
- "*Poverty and loneliness are key factors to consider*": Zoë Mohan, Mahnaz Khomamizadeh, Joyce M. Li, and Paula A. Rochon, "What's Old Is New Again: Affordable, Community-Based Housing Options for Older Women," *Journal of the American Geriatrics Society* 73, no. 3 (October 22, 2024): 982–985, online.
- *In 2021, the Commonwealth Fund Survey on Older Adults*: Canadian Institute for Health Information, "How Canada Compares: Results from the Commonwealth Fund's 2021 International Health Policy Survey of Older Adults in 11 Countries," CIHI, 2021, online.
- *In a blunt summation of what awaits*: Women's Age Lab, "Women at the Forefront of Aging in Canada."

Chapter Thirteen: Elizabeth

- *Not to be a killjoy*: Ariana Bendix, "Sexually Transmitted Infection Rates Have Risen Sharply Among Adults 55 and Older, CDC Data Shows," NBC News, March 27, 2024, online.

Chapter Fourteen: The Lodestar

- *For the entirety of their lives, most people want to be held*: Katrina Clarke, "Women's Orgasms Are Even More Fascinating Than We Fathomed," CBC Life, July 5, 2017, online.
- *Much like eating chocolate*: Martin Portner, "The Orgasmic Mind: The Neurological Roots of Sexual Pleasure," *Scientific American*, April 1, 2008, online.
- *This includes a large AARP survey on sexuality*: *Ageless Desire: Relationships and Sex in Middle Age and Beyond* (AARP Research, 2023).
- *Those who rebelled risked the hysteria diagnosis*: Kiera Boyle, "Hysterical Victorian Women," *Historic UK History Magazine*, online.
- *Today, as technological transformation threatens*: Daniel Cox, "Why Young Men Are Turning Against Feminism," Survey Center on American Life, December 14, 2023, online.
- "*There's no expiration dates for women*": Quinci LeGardye, "Salma Hayek Reminds Us That She Doesn't Age," *Harper's Bazaar*, September 3, 2021, online.
- *For years now, 80-year-old men*: Kelly Burch, "Cialis vs. Viagra: Which Is More Effective?" Verywell Health, October 1, 2024, online.

Chapter Fifteen: Pat

- *In its third annual national housing survey*: "2024 Survey Highlights the Ripples Effect of the Housing Crisis," Habitat for Humanity Canada, November 12, 2024, online.

Chapter Sixteen: Home

- *While the idea of older women sharing a home is not new*: "Census Family Status and Household Living Arrangements, Household Type of Person, Age Group and Gender: Canada, Provinces and Territories, Census Metropolitan Areas and Census Agglomerations," Statistics Canada, July 13, 2022, online.
- *I've written extensively on the value of NORC programs*: Moira Welsh, "Are You Going to Die Alone? Be a Burden to Your Family? In New York

They Do Aging Better. Why Is Ontario Missing the Obvious?" *Toronto Star*, November 4, 2022, online.

- *In 2023, Scotiabank economist Rebekah Young called on Canada*: Rebekah Young, "Canadian Housing Affordability Hurts," Scotiabank, January 18, 2023, online.
- *Nearly 100 years ago, housing captured the attention*: Patricia Begin, *Homelessness*. Library of Parliament, Parliamentary Research Branch, 1999, online.
- *Condo investors played a role in the financialization of housing*: Martine August, *The Financialization of Housing in Canada: A Summary Report for the Office of the Federal Housing Advocate*. The Office of the Federal Housing Advocate, 2022, online.
- *Among millennials and Generation X*: Daniel A. Cox, Kelsey Eyre Hammond, and Kyle Gray, "Generation Z and the Transformation of American Adolescence: How Gen Z's Formative Experiences Shape Its Politics, Priorities, and Future," Survey Center on American Life, November 9, 2023, online.

Chapter Seventeen: Onward

- *A few years ago, a young British singer-songwriter named Paris Paloma*: Paris Paloma, "Labour [Official Video]," YouTube, March 23, 2023, online.
- *Maybe it is a wary recognition*: Paris Paloma, "LABOUR [Live on Tour]," YouTube, May 29, 2025, online.
- *Starting CPP at the age of 60 instead of waiting until 70*: Rob Carrick, "One Woman's Crusade to Help People Make Better Decisions on Starting CPP Retirement Benefits," *The Globe and Mail*, April 10, 2024, online; Bonnie-Jeanne MacDonald, Doug Chandler, and Barbara Sanders, "Step #7: Strengthening CPP/QPP for Better Outcomes — Two Evidence-Based Reforms," National Institute on Ageing, Toronto Metropolitan University, December 2024, online.
- *For today's retired women, the* average *payment*: *Employment and Social Development Canada's 2023 to 2024 Departmental Results Report*. Employment and Social Development Canada, 2024, online.
- *When I first wrote about the impoverishment of older women*: Moira Welsh, "They Had Families, Worked Hard and Grew Old. Now They Face Their Final Years in Poverty. Why Are We Failing Older Women in Canada?" *Toronto Star*, March 16, 2023, online.

- *In late 2024, I wrote another piece on the gender pension gap*: Moira Welsh, "Her Pension Wasn't Enough to Cover Toronto Rent. Then She Found a Lifeline in a Different Kind of Housing." *Toronto Star*, December 24, 2024, online.
- *Roughly five months after his April 28 election*: Canada, Office of the Prime Minister, "Prime Minister Carney Launches Build Canada Homes to Supercharge Homebuilding across the Country," news release, September 14, 2025, online.
- *As the University Health Network's NORC Innovation Centre found*: NORC Innovation Centre, *A Home Care Model for Naturally Occurring Retirement Communities in Ontario*. University Health Network, 2024, online.
- *As housing expert Tim Richter wrote*: Tim Richter, "Build Canada Homes: A Promising Step — If We Get It Right," Canadian Alliance to End Homelessness, August 13, 2025, online.
- *While we know that women are increasingly*: Email to author from Josh Shanahan, March 11, 2025.
- *Every year, the Mercer CFA Global Pension Index examines*: David Knox, "Mercer CFA Institute Global Pension Index 2024," Mercer, 2024, online.
- *Many Canadians believe that older adults can simply boost*: Paloma Griffin and Mohy Tabb, *A Fine Line: Finding the Right Seniors' Poverty Measure in Canada*. Maytree, 2023, online.
- *Among the 22 percent of Canadian renters*: "2022 Canadian Housing Survey: New Insights into Housing Needs and Conditions," CMHC and Statistics Canada, September 10, 2024, online.
- *A 2023 NIA survey found that just one in seven*: B.-J. MacDonald and D. Chandler. "Step #4: Providing the Right Information in the Right Way: Removing the Biases in CPP/QPP Communications and Empowering Informed Decisions," National Institute on Ageing, Toronto Metropolitan University, 2024, online.

Entertainment. Writing. Culture.

ECW is a proudly independent, Canadian-owned book publisher. We know great writing can improve people's lives, and we're passionate about sharing original, exciting, and insightful writing across genres.

Thanks for reading along!

We want our books not just to sustain our imaginations, but to help construct a healthier, more just world, and so we've become a certified B Corporation, meaning we meet a high standard of social and environmental responsibility — and we're going to keep aiming higher. We believe books can drive change, but the way we make them can too.

Certified B Corporation

Being a B Corp means that the act of publishing this book should be a force for good — for the planet, for our communities, and for the people that worked to make this book. For example, everyone who worked on this book was paid at least a living wage. You can learn more at the Ontario Living Wage Network.

This book is also available as a Global Certified Accessible™ (GCA) ebook. ECW Press's ebooks are screen reader friendly and are built to meet the needs of those who are unable to read standard print due to blindness, low vision, dyslexia, or a physical disability.

This book is printed on FSC®-certified paper. It contains recycled materials, and other controlled sources, is processed chlorine free, and is manufactured using biogas energy.

FSC www.fsc.org MIX Paper | Supporting responsible forestry FSC® C103567

ECW's office is situated on land that was the traditional territory of many nations, including the Wendat, the Anishinaabeg, Haudenosaunee, Chippewa, Métis, and current treaty holders the Mississaugas of the Credit. In the 1880s, the land was developed as part of a growing community around St. Matthew's Anglican and other churches. Starting in the 1950s, our neighbourhood was transformed by immigrants fleeing the Vietnam War and Chinese Canadians dispossessed by the building of Nathan Phillips Square and the subsequent rise in real estate value in other Chinatowns. We are grateful to those who cared for the land before us and are proud to be working amidst this mix of cultures.

ecwpress.com